W9-AAR-624

3 1257 01524

Schaumburg Township District Library

130 South Roselle Road
Schaumburg, Illinois 60193

everyday chinese cooking
cooking

everyday
chinese
cooking

Quick and Delicious Recipes from the Leeann Chin Restaurants

SCHAUMBURG TOWNSHIP DISTRICT LIBRARY
130 SOUTH ROSELLE ROAD
SCHAUMBURG, ILLINOIS 60193

Leeann Chin and Katie Chin

Clarkson Potter/Publishers
New York

641.5951
CHI

3 1257 01324 5450

Copyright © 2000 by Leeann Chin and Katie Chin

All rights reserved. No part of this book may be reproduced or transmitted in any form or by any means, electronic or mechanical, including photocopying, recording, or by any information storage and retrieval system, without permission in writing from the publisher.

Published by Clarkson Potter/Publishers, New York, New York. Member of the Crown Publishing Group.

Random House, Inc. New York, Toronto, London, Sydney, Auckland
www.randomhouse.com

Clarkson N. Potter is a trademark and POTTER and colophon are registered trademarks of Random House, Inc.

Printed in the United States of America

Design by Jan Derevjanik

Library of Congress Cataloging-in-Publication Data
Chin, Leeann.
   Everyday Chinese cooking: quick and delicious recipes from the Leeann Chin Restaurants / by Leeann Chin and Katie Chin — 1st ed.   1. Cookery, Chinese.
I. Chin, Katie.   II. Title.
TX724.5.C5 C561163   2000
641.5951—dc21   00-020900

ISBN 0-609-60586-0

10   9   8   7   6   5   4   3   2   1

First Edition

To Leeann's grandchildren:
Siu Ping, Dai Wai, Wai Lee,
Rutledge, Logan, Little Katie,
and Griffin—the next
generation of Chin-family cooks!

acknowledgments

We would like to thank Julia Molino for making this happen; our wonderful editors, Katie Workman and Chris Pavone, for their support and guidance; our art director, Marysarah Quinn, for her incredible eye and spirit; and the terrific staff at Clarkson Potter, who put this project together.

We would also like to thank our family and friends for their continued support and for acting as our testers at countless dinner parties; Michele and Sharon for their hard work and dedication; Billy and Scott for their input and inspiration; and, finally, all of Leeann's customers, whose continued loyalty has motivated us all along the way,

contents

everyday chinese

cooking

preface

Welcome to *Everyday Chinese Cooking*! Many people are intimidated by the thought of Chinese cooking at home. Many of the customers who visit my restaurants, as well as friends of my daughter Katie, voice the same concerns: "There are too many exotic ingredients," "What about all that preparation?" "I love Chinese food, but I really don't have the time to make it." It became very clear to us that there was a need for a cookbook filled with simple recipes you can make in your own kitchen using easily available ingredients and your very own pots, pans, and utensils.

Chinese cooking, for the most part, is extremely healthful. Our recipes yield low-calorie/low-fat meals by using less oil than you might expect. Nonstick pans and vegetable-based oil sprays have made it easier to use a lighter hand with cooking fat and get excellent results. We will also share with the reader the "yin and yang" philosophy in Chinese cooking: how to use this basic principle of balance in cooking to create delicious and nutritious meals for your friends and family.

Today, it's much easier to find an array of Asian ingredients at the grocery store. You will see that many of the same basic ingredients are used consistently in Chinese cooking, enabling you to keep a well-stocked kitchen for quick and easy Chinese meals. For those times when you are in a pinch, we've also included several recommendations for substitutions, so a missing ingredient doesn't prevent you from whipping up a wonderful Chinese meal.

Most people think they must use a wok to make Chinese recipes. In this book, we will teach you how to use a simple frying pan or skillet to create tasty Sichuan stir-fry dishes, your oven to create wonderfully smoked fish fillets, and a simple pot to steam light and healthful vegetable dumplings.

And we also want our readers to learn that Chinese cooking is a family affair. Involve your loved ones in the process to make the whole experience fulfilling—I often have my grandchildren over to make dumplings and noodles with me. They love to knead the stretchy dough and make interesting and creative shapes. Our recipes are meant to be shared "family style" and it is in this tradition that we encourage your family and friends to participate and make cooking fun.

Most of the time involved in Chinese cooking is in advance preparation. We will show you how to plan ahead and save time, so a few minutes of work in the morning will lead to dinner in 10 to 15 minutes when you return home from work. Many of our recipes can be made in larger batches, enabling you to freeze smaller portions for future meals. For example, I have taught my daughter to freeze packages of stir-fried chicken. When she comes home, she merely tosses the meat in a wok or skillet with some fresh vegetables and she has a healthy and satisfying dinner in minutes.

If you're like Katie, planning for dinner, much less a dinner party, can sometimes be a stressful experience. We'll show you how easy it is to plan ahead with Chinese cooking. We'll share many of our methods for preparing certain parts of the meal beforehand, like marinating Mongolian-style beef before you leave for work to broiling chicken wings the day before a dinner party, allowing you to relax and simply reheat just as your guests are arriving.

Chinese people love to entertain and our family is no exception. Learn how to impress your friends with a few tricks, like adding a caviar garnish to traditional Chinese spring rolls to create an elegant first course. Learn how to host a formal Chinese New Year's banquet by following my suggested menu planning, or throw a last-minute cocktail party for your friends featuring several fun and delicious appetizers.

By combining my experience as a chef/restaurateur and my daughter's perspective as a busy career woman, our goal is to teach you the basic techniques found in Chinese cooking and show you that Chinese cooking can truly become part of your everyday lifestyle.

Please enjoy this book as much as we enjoyed working on it together. It is a true celebration of our cultural heritage and we hope our recipes will bring your family and friends together as much as they have for us.

Leeann Chin

introduction

Born Wai-Hing, my mother grew up working for her father's grocery store in Canton. She was constantly surrounded by the sights, smells, and sounds of a bustling marketplace filled with the greenest and leafiest produce, fragrant lychee nuts, glistening sea bass, clucking hens, and carts filled with steaming dumplings. She followed her family's chef around with wide-eyed fascination as he masterfully drew from her family's rich selection of vegetables and meats to create simple yet delicious, beautifully prepared meals for her family. Soon she was creating her own recipes and earned the job of chief assistant to the chef.

At the same time, she had to deliver fifty-pound rice bags on her bike as well as master the abacus for customers (not customary tasks for a young girl). For this, she became regarded as a tomboy and was treated by her parents with little regard or concern. Her early childhood experiences fueled both her rebellious spirit as well as her love of cooking.

When she was seventeen, her parents sent her to Hong Kong to meet my father. It was an arranged marriage and she had to adapt to a new life very quickly. She went from the comfort and familiarity of a large family and bountiful surroundings to suddenly being thrust into a new life with a husband she barely knew and a stern and demanding mother-in-law. She tried as best she could to adjust to the bright lights and crowds of the big city, to settle into their dusty, cramped apartment, and to accept her new role in life: to serve and respect her husband. Although her cooking never seemed good enough to please her mother-in-law *or* my father, she continued to experiment with new recipes and was delighted by the exotic new ingredients and methods Hong Kong had to offer.

In 1956, my parents boarded a ship bound for Minnesota and my mother, Wai-Hing, knew her life would never be the same. She adapted as best she could, but she could barely find rice or even fresh garlic at the supermarket. Yet my father still expected my mother to re-create the authentic dishes he craved from their homeland.

My mother learned how to improvise and relied on the main guiding philosophy taught by her family chef in China: Use the freshest ingredients available and seek balance in creating dishes (a.k.a. the yin and yang of cooking). Soon, Leeann (her newly picked American name) was experimenting with trout, Cornish game hen, and other foods indigenous to the United States, realizing that she could still prepare delicious everyday meals in her new American kitchen without compromising the integrity of her cooking. She realized that her avocado green Amana Radar range could achieve the high heat levels required for Chinese cooking and even discovered that a frying pan could easily substitute for a wok.

Coming to America brought the promise of a better life for our family. It also brought the challenges of instilling a sense of cultural pride in all of my brothers and sisters while encouraging us to assimilate into American society. Like most children raised in the '60s and '70s, we craved macaroni and cheese, hot dogs, pizza, and Rice-a-Roni. My mother relented on Friday nights when my father went off to play cards at our uncle Jack's house.

During the rest of the week, however, we'd run home to "Sik fan" (eat dinner) together, devouring my mother's dishes scooped over steaming hot bowls of white rice. She saw how we craved the simple, yet delicious flavors of stir-fried chicken with vegetables or five-ingredient fried rice and realized we would gladly eat our vegetables as long as they were dancing among the delicate pieces of velvety chicken my mother expertly prepared.

She took care in all the ingredients she selected and even though my family was on a very tight budget, she always made us feel like we were special every night around our kitchen table as we ate barbecued duck, sizzling rice soup, orange-flavored beef, and sub-gum stir-fry. We savored every bite.

My mother was supplementing the household income by working as a seamstress out of our home for local neighborhood clients.

One day in 1973, she threw a luncheon for her sewing customers. They were so impressed with her cooking, they encouraged her to start teaching cooking classes. Before long, she was teaching and catering all over the Minneapolis–St. Paul area. Through word of mouth, her cooking attracted the attention of Sean Connery as well as the owner of the Minnesota Twins, both of whom decided to invest in her first restaurant in 1983. A cookbook soon followed and then several more restaurants and carry-out locations.

In 1985, she sold her business to General Mills. She bought her company back in 1988 to maintain her personal vision and grow the business herself. Today, there are more than fifty Leeann Chin restaurants and take-out locations.

In talking with her restaurant clientele over the years, my mother realized there was a need for a cookbook focusing on everyday Chinese cooking. She began to recognize that people have so little time or energy these days, they need a resource to teach them how to create simple, quick meals using traditional Chinese methods.

Then, on a recent trip to Los Angeles, my mother went exploring in *my* refrigerator to find only a half pint of Häagen-Dazs and some ice. She realized then that I—her own daughter—needed a resource to incorporate Chinese cooking into my hectic lifestyle. My work as an entertainment executive left me little time to cook, and because of this I often ate out or ordered in.

By working on this project together, my mother has taught me the basic techniques and preparations to make Chinese cooking easy and fun—for example, how easy it is to cook larger portions ahead of time and store smaller amounts for quick meals. Now my refrigerator and freezer are chock-full of packets of blanched vegetables, precut and precooked shrimp and chicken pieces, as well as noodles and rice. After a long day at the office, I can quickly toss a couple of bags into the microwave and then into my nonstick frying pan and presto: a home-cooked dinner.

Please join us as we share in the secrets and family traditions my mother treasures from her childhood in China as well as the memories my mother and I have shared growing up together in America.

Katie Chin

glossary of ingredients

pantry

baby corn
Miniature ears of corn often used in stir-fried dishes. They come canned and ready to cook.

bamboo shoots
The young edible shoots of certain bamboo plants. They are eaten as a vegetable. The canned variety is readily available—they come whole, sliced, or in chunks. Fresh ones may be hard to find and are much more expensive.

bean curd, fermented red
Tofu preserved with rice wine and spices is sold in jars in Chinese grocery stores. It can be used as an accompaniment or in cooking and will keep indefinitely.

bean curd skins
This delightful, chewy pastalike substance is made from dried tofu. It comes in strips or sheets.

black beans, fermented
These are fermented salted black soybeans, which have a distinctive pungent aroma, adding a very rich flavor when combined with garlic, ginger, and other flavors. They come packed in plastic bags or made into sauces, sold in jars. They should be rinsed in warm water before using to remove excess salt. Refrigerate after opening.

black mushrooms
Dried; must be soaked before using. They come in a wide variety of grades, with prices to match. They also are known in Japanese as shiitake mushrooms (especially the lighter brown variety).

brown bean paste

The ground version of brown beans, used in sauces. A thick, salty, and rich cousin of black bean sauce, it can be purchased in a jar.

brown beans

A rich and pungent addition to Chinese dishes. Whole beans should be mashed before using. Refrigerate after opening.

cayenne

Ground dried red pepper and very hot. It can be used in place of chili paste in a pinch.

chicken stock

Available canned, but of course freshly prepared stock is better.

chilies, dried red

These are dried red peppers and usually very hot. They are an essential ingredient in many Sichuan dishes and can be used to season oil.

chili paste

Made from crushed fresh red chilies, soybeans, salt, and garlic, it varies from being hot to very hot. Sold in jars, it is used in cooking and as a condiment. You can make your own by combining 1 tablespoon vegetable oil, 1 teaspoon minced garlic, 1 teaspoon chopped ginger, ½ cup brown bean sauce, 1 teaspoon cayenne, and 1 tablespoon sugar and stir-frying for about 10 minutes over medium-low heat.

cloud ears

Also known as Chinese tree fungus, they come dried and should be soaked for 20 minutes before using; any hard portions should be trimmed. They then swell up to look like little clouds. They have a mild smoky flavor.

coconut milk

Used chiefly as a sauce ingredient in Southeast Asian dishes and desserts, it comes canned. Lower-fat versions are commonly available. Do not substitute sweetened coconut cream.

cornstarch

Used to thicken sauces and in marinades, it is a very important ingredient that should always be kept in your pantry. When mixed with a small amount of water, the paste is added to broth to make savory stir-fry sauces. It is often used to coat meats before stir-frying or deep-frying in order to seal in the flavors and to cook more crisply. Available everywhere. Substitutes include arrowroot and potato starch, but never wheat flour.

curry powder

An English term for a blend of common Indian spices. Quality and flavor can vary widely, so it is worth shopping around.

fish sauce

A Vietnamese sauce made of fish and seafood essences, it is used in cooking or as a condiment.

five-spice powder

As the name suggests, this is a combination of five ground spices: star anise, Sichuan pepper, fennel, cloves, and cinnamon. Complexly pungent and spicy with a hint of sweetness, it can be found in Asian stores.

hoisin sauce

A dark reddish-brown sweet and salty sauce made with soy mash, vinegar, sugar, and flavorings, it is often used to flavor roasted meat and poultry dishes. It may be also used as a condiment and purchased in a jar or canned.

lotus seed paste

Made from ground lotus seeds, it is often used in savory dishes and sweetened to fill buns and pastry.

lychees

Mildly sweet in flavor, they are available fresh or canned. Fresh lychees, berrylike fruit encased in a brown and pink shell, are becoming more common in Asian markets. The canned variety is widely available.

mandarin oranges

Canned, little sweetened oranges.

mango

Sweetened alternative in a jar to fresh mango.

miso, light

Japanese fermented soybean paste. Much lighter than the Chinese version, it is used in soups and sauces. The light variety is called shiro miso, as opposed to the dark aka miso.

mustard, dried

Mixed with water or vinegar to make a hot dipping condiment, often with appetizers. Also known as Chinese or English mustard.

noodles

A major staple throughout Asia, they are made chiefly of either wheat or rice flour, and are fresh, frozen, or dried. There is a large variety sold in Asian supermarkets. They come in many different shapes and are served in many different ways. When eggs are added to wheat flour, they are called egg noodles and are panfried or used in soups. Rice sticks are made of rice flour and must be soaked before using. They puff up when deep-fried and are used as a garnish. Bean threads are made from mung beans and are sometimes called cellophane noodles. When they are deep-fried, they puff up dramatically.

nuts

Almonds, peanuts, walnuts, and pine nuts are used in cooked dishes. They are often pan-roasted first.

plum sauce

At once both sweet and sour, it is used as a dipping sauce for spring rolls and barbecued meats.

rice paper

Paper-thin translucent sheets made of rice flour, salt, and water used for making Vietnamese-style spring rolls.

rices

There are many kinds of rice eaten in Asia. The most common Chinese rice is long-grain white rice. Jasmine and basmati are less starchy and more nutty in fragrance. Japanese rice is short-grain and more glutinous and sweeter. Sticky (also known as glutinous or sweet) rice or Thai black sticky rice can be used in desserts. While many consider brown rice to be more healthful, Asians usually stick to white rice. (By analogy, note that Europeans do not eat whole wheat baguettes and whole wheat pasta.)

rice wine

Used in cooking. Look for the label "Shaoxing." You may substitute dry sherry, but not the Japanese sake or mirin, which are sweeter.

scallops, dried

A delicacy used in soups and other dishes, they might resemble thin noodles or threads when cooked.

sesame oil

Used as a seasoning in many dishes.

soy sauce

Comes in three grades: light, medium, and dark. Dark soy tends to be used in cooking, while the lighter kinds are used more for dipping. One delicious and popular version is mushroom soy. Beware of low-grade artificially colored and flavored grocery store brands. Soy sauces can be stored at room temperature.

star anise

The eight-pointed seed pod whose flavor resembles Western anise (though not botanically related). Sometimes called five-star anise, it is often used in slow-cooked dishes and for flavoring teas.

straw mushrooms

Available canned in Asian groceries.

turmeric

The deeply yellow-colored, bitter, and pungent spice is ground from a root that is related to ginger. It is a component of curry powder.

water chestnuts

Available canned or fresh, these bulbs of the Asian marsh have a delicate flavor and add a crunchy texture to stir-fried dishes and soups. The fresh ones must be peeled and washed. An interesting alternative is pared jicama root.

white pepper

A variant of ordinary black pepper is of course whitish, with a sharper but lighter taste. White peppercorns are commonly available.

produce

asian pears

Also known by the name pear apple or Japanese pear, it is a yellow-skinned fruit that is crisp, light, delicately sweet, and lives up to one of its names: It is shaped like an apple, but tastes somewhat like a pear. As a snack, it is a real treat.

asparagus

An elegant stir-fry ingredient. For an extra nice touch, the stems can be peeled.

basil

A celebrated aromatic herb typically used in Thai recipes. There are several types available in Asian markets.

bean sprouts

Mung bean sprouts are perhaps the most common. They are crunchy when near raw, but wilt quickly under boiling heat. They last for only a couple of days in the refrigerator. Soy sprouts are larger and crunchier and should not be eaten raw. Both varieties are used in stir-fried dishes, omelets, and salads.

bell peppers

The red and green ones make a colorful addition to many dishes. Often they can just be heated through, just barely cooked. The seeds and bitter membranes should be removed before cooking.

bok choy

A crisp vegetable shaped roughly like a celery plant, it has whitish stalks and deep green leaves. The smaller they are, the more tender and the littlest ones, called baby bok choy, are expensive. Bok choy can be found in most supermarkets. As for any vegetable, freshness counts. One common variant, Shanghai bok choy, which can be found in many Asian markets, is uniformly pearly green in color and slightly bitter; the baby ones are highly prized.

broccoli

First, cut off the florets, then peel the stems and cut off the butt. Chinese broccoli (kale) is not broccoli, but a vaguely similar vegetable called *gai lan*. It has crunchy, thin stems and slightly bitter deep green leaves. This vegetable is commonly eaten by Chinese in restaurants and is highly nutritional.

carrots

Skilled carvers turn carrots into exotic garnishes shaped like phoenixes and dragons. You could try this too, or you can just slice them or shred them into matchsticks. Carrots are also a well-known source of vitamin A, and some would say that they make you a nicer person.

celery

An easy-to-use vegetable that can be used in many dishes. Artfully sliced layers of celery can make a nice garnish.

chilies

Used to provide heat. The most common variety is slender and measures 2 to 3 inches in length. Jalapeños are green and plump, and usually pack more of a punch. Thai chilies are tiny red peppers, measuring less than an inch, and are even more powerful.

chinese long beans

Also known as yard long beans, they can be up to that long. They are sold coiled or tied into bunches, and are cooked roughly like the similar (though unrelated) green beans; they can be blanched and/or stir-fried.

chives

Rich and earthy yet delicate, these relatives of the garlic plant are a delicious onionlike vegetable. Chinese chives are similar to Western chives, but stronger and coarser; the less common Chinese yellow chives are more delicate in flavor. Nearby these Chinese chives you might find the related and similar garlic shoots and garlic chives.

cilantro

Also known as fresh coriander (and by the obsolete "Chinese parsley"), it resembles Italian parsley with flat leaves, but with a unique sharp musky flavor. It is used in many dishes as a garnish or wilted into sauces and soups.

cucumber

We prefer the European or English cucumber. Slice thin and layer around the edge of a serving platter for an elegant garnish for fish or cold meats.

daikon radish

Also known as Chinese white radish, it is long and white, shaped like a gargantuan carrot. It is treated as a root vegetable and thus commonly boiled. It can be shredded for use in salads or as a garnish.

eggplant

See Squashes.

egg roll wrappers

Made of pliable wheat dough, they are large square (usually about 7 to 8 inches) wrappers for spring rolls. Sold fresh or frozen, they are stuffed with chopped fillings and deep-fried.

eggs

Always keep this basic and highly nutritional source on hand. They keep for a long time and are used in many Asian recipes.

garlic

A must for your produce shelf, it is minced, sliced, left whole, fried, boiled, and used in every conceivable way. Perhaps the most common use is to fry it and thereby flavor the oil, which is used further. It is an absolutely essential ingredient. Go out and get some now!

gingerroot

Another absolute must for your produce shelf. The fresh root is pungent, spicy, and aromatic. It must be peeled and then is usually smashed with the blade of a cleaver (or chef's knife) before being chopped or slivered. Keep in a paper bag in the refrigerator for best results. Peeled ginger can be preserved by covering with dry sherry or rice wine. The flavored liquid can naturally be used for cooking as well.

green beans

Used in stir-fried dishes and often paired with pork. The ends should be broken off this common vegetable before washing and cooking. French-style green beans are a more tender variant and have the advantage of having edible ends. The common vegetable is similar to the Chinese long bean (see page 23).

green onions

Also known as scallions or spring onions, they are a common vegetable in Chinese dishes. They should not be overcooked and are often used as a raw garnish.

lemons and limes

Juiced or sliced, they can be added to sweet-and-sour and other sauces. Also used as a garnish.

lotus root

Beige and oblong, it is actually the root of the lotus flower. When sliced, it reveals a surprising system of baffles and chambers. It can be used to add crunch in salads, soups, and braised dishes, or it can be eaten raw or briefly stir-fried. It should be peeled and sliced. Lotus root can be bought at Asian grocery stores.

mango

The succulent sweet fruit. The skin is a mixture of green, orange, and yellow, and it is deeply orange and very juicy on the inside. It can be sliced, scored, and eaten right off the skin. It can also be peeled, pitted, and used in desserts. Fresh mangos are now readily available throughout the year.

mint leaves

These herbs are used in spicy Southeast Asian dishes, often accompanied by spices. They are also used in fish dishes and soups.

mushrooms

Among the many varieties now available you will find the enoki, oyster, shiitake, and the common white mushroom. Enokis are tiny with long stems that make them seem almost like noodles. Shiitakes are brown in color, round, and flat, with meaty rich flavor. Normally only the caps are eaten, as the stems can be chewy. Oyster mushrooms are vaguely redolent of oysters and have a leafy irregular shape. All mushrooms should be wiped well with a damp paper towel before using. Fresh mushrooms have a milder and altogether different flavor than their dried counterparts; they are definitely not interchangeable (though both are delicious).

napa cabbage

Also called celery cabbage. Mild and crunchy, this pale green leafy vegetable absorbs flavors well, and can be stir-fried, braised, or used in soups. Avoid shriveled leaves, but don't worry about the little black spots that may appear near the base.

noodles, fresh

Made of wheat or rice flour, fresh or frozen noodles in an assortment of shapes, textures, and consistencies can be found in Asian supermarkets.

onions

Usually diced and included in many stir-fried meat dishes. The most common variety is the yellow onion, available everywhere. To avoid tears, learn to keep your head away from the offending vapors when you cut them. Believe me, it can be easily done with practice.

shallots

Resembling small reddish onions or large garlic bulbs, they are actually mild-mannered members of the onion family. They are sweetly aromatic and readily available, but sometimes pricey. This cross between onion and garlic is used widely in China.

siu mai wrappers

These round sheets of pasta are made of the same wheat dough used to make wonton wrappers. They are typically used to make siu mai and other dumplings, such as potstickers. The dumplings are deep-fried, panfried, or steamed.

snow peas

The flat, tender, yet crispy edible pea pods. The ends and the fibrous strings running along one side should be pulled off. They are frequently used in stir-fries and soups and are a particularly fetching partner for shrimp. Avoid discolored pods and make sure that you use them within a few days.

spring roll wrappers

Similar to egg roll wrappers but thinner and translucent, they are stuffed with chopped fillings and are cooked in a variety of ways. They are sold fresh or frozen.

squashes

There are quite a variety of squashes. The most common one, zucchini, is easy to prepare and cooks quickly. Acorn and butternut squashes are similar to pumpkin and are essentially interchangeable; both have hard skins and must be peeled. They cook quickly and can be stir-fried. A variety of eggplants can be used in strong-flavored dishes. The diminutive Japanese eggplant and tiny Thai eggplant are now commonly available. The thinner you slice squash varieties, the quicker they will cook.

sugar snap peas

Similar to snow peas. The pods are completely edible, but the ends and stringy fibers need to be removed. Unlike snow peas, they contain small peas within the pod. They keep for about a week, refrigerated in plastic.

tofu

Also known as bean curd, it is pronounced *doh fu* (or *dow fu*) in Chinese (Cantonese). Made from ground soybeans formed into a custardlike slab, it comes in a variety of textures. Its taste might best be described as being aggressively bland, though it is good at absorbing flavors. High in protein and other nutrients, it is the best nonanimal protein source. It should keep up to five days refrigerated, provided you change the water daily.

tomatoes

A fairly common yet somewhat modern ingredient in Chinese dishes (tomatoes have been eaten in Asia for at least 100 years), especially in stir-fried dishes and some soups. Most native Chinese do not regard it as a foreign fruit or vegetable. They can be sculpted to make attractive garnishes, e.g., in the shape of a rose.

wonton wrappers

These square sheets of pasta are made of wheat flour and egg, the same dough used to make egg roll wrappers. They are used to wrap minced meat, seafood, and vegetables. The wontons can be deep-fried, panfried, steamed, or boiled in soups. The wrappers come fresh or frozen in piles of thirty or forty, wrapped in plastic.

appetizers

Bean Curd Rolls

Beef with Scallops

Crystal Dumplings

Chilled Spring Rolls with Smoked Salmon

Chilled Vegetable Spring Rolls

Chicken Skewers

Crispy Shrimp Wrapped in Bacon

Fish Cakes

Garlic Chicken Wings

Honey-Glazed Spareribs

Lettuce Cups with Turkey

Panfried Pork Dumplings

Firecracker Shrimp

Siu Mai

Spicy Beef Skewers

Steamed Shrimp Rolls

Thousand-Corner Shrimp Balls

Tofu and Shrimp Medallions

Scallop Skewers

Scallops Wrapped with Bacon

Sea Legs Wrapped in Shrimp and Tofu

Vegetable Dumplings

bean curd rolls

makes 16 rolls

Fresh bean curd sheets can be found at Asian markets. These rolls can be completely made ahead and resteamed. You can also save the steaming step for later and store the uncooked rolls in the refrigerator.

8	ounces medium shrimp, deveined	2	green onions
1	teaspoon salt	8	ounces bean sprouts
1	teaspoon sesame oil	2	tablespoons vegetable oil
4	bean curd sheets	1	cup Chicken Broth (page 52) or Vegetable
½	cup all-purpose flour		Broth (page 54)
2	ounces shiitake mushrooms	2	tablespoons oyster sauce
2	ounces bamboo shoots		

Cut the shrimp lengthwise into halves. In a small bowl, mix the salt and 2 cups water. Place the shrimp in the salt water for 5 minutes, then rinse with cold water, drain, and pat dry with paper towels. Mix the shrimp with the sesame oil and set aside.

Cut each bean curd sheet into quarters, forming 4 wedges. Using a wet towel, wipe off both sides of the bean curd sheet. Mix the flour with ½ cup cold water to make a paste for sealing the bean curd rolls.

Rinse the shiitake mushrooms with cold water. Cut off and discard the stems. Cut the mushrooms into ⅛-inch strips. Cut the bamboo shoots into ⅛-inch-thin strips. Shred the green onions, including the tops, into thin strips.

In a bowl, mix the shrimp, mushrooms, bamboo shoots, green onions, and bean sprouts. Separate the filling into 16 portions and place each portion of filling on the widest part of the bean curd wedge. Spread out the filling about 1 inch from each edge. Start rolling the sheet and filling into a tight 4-inch roll from the widest edge. Fold in the remaining 2 corners on top of the roll and continue to roll up. Brush the flour/water mixture on the edge of the sheet and roll to seal.

Heat a skillet over high heat and add the vegetable oil. Place the rolls in the skillet and panfry for 2 to 3 minutes, turning to brown all sides. Add the chicken broth to the pan and cook until boiling. Reduce the heat to medium, cover, and steam the bean curd rolls for 2 minutes. Add the oyster sauce. Continue cooking until all the broth is absorbed, about 3 minutes. Remove the rolls from the pan and cut each roll into 4 pieces. Place on a platter and serve.

28   everyday chinese cooking

beef with scallops

Do the preparation ahead of time and broil just before the guests arrive. Great for company, this is an impressive appetizer that goes well with stir-fry dishes.

dipping sauce

4	tablespoons hoisin sauce
2	tablespoons balsamic vinegar

10	large scallops (about 1 pound)
8	ounces flank steak
½	teaspoon salt
¼	teaspoon white pepper
1	teaspoon cornstarch
4	tablespoons vegetable oil
4	garlic cloves, smashed and peeled

To make a dipping sauce, in a small bowl, mix together the hoisin sauce and vinegar and set aside.

Remove the muscles on the side of each scallop, rinse with cold water, and pat dry with paper towels. Cut the flank steak across the grain into paper-thin slices. Sprinkle the salt, pepper, and cornstarch over the beef slices. Wrap each scallop with sliced beef all the way around each scallop. Use toothpicks to secure the end of the beef slice into each scallop.

Heat a wok or large skillet over high heat; add the oil and garlic. Add the beef-wrapped scallops. Fry until both sides are browned, 2 to 3 minutes. Remove from the pan and serve with the dipping sauce.

crystal dumplings

makes about 40 dumplings

Guests love this easy and healthy appetizer. Keep frozen wonton wrappers on hand in the freezer. Wonton wrappers can be found at Asian markets and some grocery stores.

2½	teaspoons salt, divided
1	pound shrimp, deveined
1	teaspoon sugar
¼	teaspoon white pepper
1	teaspoon sesame oil
2	teaspoons cornstarch
2	medium egg whites, divided
½	cup chopped cilantro leaves

dipping sauce

2	tablespoons soy sauce
2	tablespoons balsamic vinegar
1	tablespoon chopped green onion, white and green parts
1	pound wonton wrappers (about 40 wrappers)
2	tablespoons vegetable oil, divided

Place 2½ cups warm water in a bowl and add 2 teaspoons salt; stir to dissolve. Place the shrimp in the salt water and swirl. Leave the shrimp in the salt water for 5 minutes, then rinse with cold water and drain. Pat dry on paper towels. Chop the shrimp into a paste (you may use a food processor).

In a medium bowl, combine the shrimp, the remaining ½ teaspoon salt, the sugar, pepper, sesame oil, cornstarch, 1 egg white, and cilantro. Mix well. Beat the remaining egg white with 1 tablespoon water for sealing the dumplings.

In a small bowl, mix the soy sauce, balsamic vinegar, and green onion to make a dipping sauce. Set aside.

Trim the wonton wrappers to form circles. Place 2 teaspoons filling in the center of the circle. Brush with the egg mixture along the edge. Fold over to form a half circle.

Heat a large, nonstick skillet over high heat. Add 1 tablespoon vegetable oil and turn the heat down to medium.

Add 20 dumplings and panfry for 1 minute. Add ½ cup water. Cover and cook 1 minute.

Remove the cover and continue to cook until the water is fully absorbed, about 2 minutes. Repeat the process until all the dumplings are cooked. Serve with the dipping sauce.

chilled spring rolls with smoked salmon

These appetizers, which can be rolled ahead of time, make light and refreshing summer appetizers. You may substitute lobster or any type of cooked seafood for the salmon. Rice paper rounds, which can be found at Asian markets, are very brittle and dry but are softened by being dipped in water. Be careful not to allow them to touch after they've been dipped in water, as they will stick together. Keep plenty on hand in your pantry for parties.

dipping sauce
½   cup white wine vinegar
½   cup sugar
1   teaspoon minced garlic
2   tablespoons fish sauce
2   small hot red peppers, seeded and thinly
     sliced
1   tablespoon minced carrots

½   Asian pear or other firm pear
24   fresh thin French green beans
8   sheets dried rice paper spring roll wrappers
     (8 inches round)
16   tender lettuce leaves (4 × 2 inches), such as
     Boston
4   ounces smoked salmon, cut into 8 slices
16   fresh mint leaves
½   ounce caviar (optional)

To prepare a dipping sauce, in a small pan, bring ½ cup water, the vinegar, sugar, and garlic to a boil and boil for 2 minutes over high heat. Add the fish sauce, sliced red peppers, and carrots. Remove from the heat and let cool. Cover and chill.

Peel the pear and cut it into 16 slices. Bring a small pot of water to a boil. Place the green beans in the boiling water, return the water to boiling, and cook for about 20 seconds. Drain the beans and rinse immediately with cold water. Set aside.

Wet 2 large kitchen towels and lay them flat on the counter. Dip each spring roll wrapper in warm water and place on the wet towel. Repeat the procedure, but do not stack the wrappers. When all the wrappers have been dipped in warm water, place 2 more damp kitchen towels on top of them. Allow the wrappers to sit for 5 minutes; always keep the wrappers moist.

Take 1 wrapper and place 1 piece of lettuce about 1 inch off center. Layer the ingredients in the following sequence: smoked salmon, 2 Asian pear pieces, 3 green beans, 2 mint leaves, and 1 more piece of lettuce. Starting with the corner closest to you, fold the end on top of the lettuce. Fold the sides in, then roll. Repeat the procedure with the remaining ingredients. Cut each roll in half. Place on a platter, cut-side up.

If desired, spoon some caviar on top of each spring roll. Serve with the chilled dipping sauce.

chilled vegetable
spring rolls

You can prepare these ahead and store them in the refrigerator, covered with plastic wrap, before serving, up to 1 hour. The sauce will remain fresh 4 to 5 weeks in the refrigerator.

dipping sauce

½   cup vinegar
½   cup sugar
1   teaspoon minced garlic
2   tablespoons fish sauce
2   thinly sliced small hot red peppers
1   tablespoon minced carrots

2   ounces bean thread noodles
8   sheets dried rice paper spring roll wrappers
    (8 inches round)
16 tender lettuce leaves (4 × 2 inches), such as
    Boston
½   Asian pear, peeled, cored, and cut into
    16 pieces
16 fresh mint leaves
1   small cucumber, peeled and cut into 16 thin
    slices

To prepare a dipping sauce, in a small saucepan, bring ½ cup water, the vinegar, sugar, and garlic to a boil. Boil for 2 minutes over high heat. Remove from heat and add the fish sauce, hot peppers, and carrots and remove from the heat. Cover and chill.

Place the bean thread noodles in a saucepan with enough water to cover and bring to a boil.

When the noodles are at a full boil, remove from the heat, immediately drain in a colander, and rinse with cold water until they are completely cooled. (Be careful not to overcook the noodles or they will become mushy.) Divide into 8 parts and set aside.

Wet 2 large kitchen towels and lay them side by side flat on the counter. Dip each rice paper wrapper in warm water and place side by side on wet towels. Repeat the procedure, but do not allow the wrappers to overlap or they will stick.

Place another large damp kitchen towel on top of them and repeat until all the wrappers are dipped. Allow the wrappers to sit for 5 minutes. Always keep the wrappers moist.

Take 1 wrapper, place 1 part cooked bean thread noodles about 1 inch off center, and spread out about 3 inches long.

Layer the ingredients in the following sequence: 1 lettuce leaf, 2 Asian pear pieces, 2 mint leaves, cucumber, and 1 lettuce leaf.

clockwise from top left:
crispy fish with ginger-scallion sauce (*page 123*);
yeung chau fried rice (*page 177*); lobster with ginger and scallions (*page 129*);
and chicken with shiitake mushrooms and snow peas (*page 78*)

1 Star Anise	11 Dried Egg Noodles (Thin)	19 Lotus Seed Paste	28 Mung Bean Noodles (Wide)	37 Black Mushrooms
2 Rice Noodles (Wide)	12 Rice Noodles (Thin)	20 Baby Corn	29 Shu Mei Skins	38 Chili Paste
3 Rice Noodles (Wide)	13 Miso	21 Mustard, Dried	30 Bean Curd Skins	39 Lychees
4 Oyster Sauce	14 Curry Powder	22 Chili Sauce	31 Rice Paper	40 Straw Mushrooms
5 Salad Dressing	15 Black Beans (Fermented)	23 Five Spice Powder	32 Eggroll Skins	41 Fermented Black Bean Curd
6 Dried Black Mushrooms	16 Plum Sauce	24 Turmeric	33 Wonton Skins	42 Jasmine Rice
7 Mung Bean Noodles (Thin)	17 Brown Bean Paste	25 Cayenne Pepper	34 Chilies, Dried Red	43 Dried Egg Noodles (Thin)
8 Sesame Oil	18 Dried Egg Noodles (Wide)	26 Brown Beans	35 Scallops (Dried)	44 Bamboo Shoots
9 Peking Sauce		27 Dried Egg Noodles (Thin)	36 Cloud Ear Mushrooms	
10 Coconut Milk				

1	Broccoli	8	Celery	15	Tomatoes	22	Garlic	29	Bean Sprouts
2	Lime	9	Squash	16	Baby Bok Choy	23	Shallots	30	Basil
3	Gingerroot	10	Chilies	17	Daikon Radish	24	Chives	31	Green Onions (Scallions)
4	Lemon	11	Bok Choy	18	Carrots	25	Cilantro	32	Enoki
5	Bell Pepper (Green)	12	Snow Peas	19	Lotus Root	26	Oyster (Fresh)	33	Mango
6	Asian Pear	13	Bell Pepper (Red)	20	Oyster (Canned)	27	Thai Chilies		
7	Napa Cabbage	14	Chinese Long Beans	21	Eggplant	28	Sugar Snap Peas		

Stir-frying Tips

It's important that all ingredients are prepared and organized when stir-frying, as the method is based on cooking
everything very fast. We encourage you to read recipes
thoroughly beforehand so you feel prepared and confident.
Stir-frying dates back centuries in China when people
cooked their meals on wood-burning stoves with extremely
hot flames.

Today, American stoves deliver high enough heat levels to
achieve the even distribution required for Chinese cooking.
A wok is ideal for stir-frying given its design, however, most
stir-fry dishes can be created just as easily in a frying pan or
Dutch oven as long as it can sustain high heat. Nonstick
frying pans are ideal for stir-fried meat and seafood dishes
and require much less oil. Whether you use a wok or frying
pan, it's important to start with a clean, dry pan. You
should also heat the pan before you add oil and make sure
it is very hot before you begin cooking. You should hear a
"sizzling" sound throughout the stir-frying process.

When stir-frying, you must use a firm spatula, which will
easily slide under the ingredients. Don't attempt to stir the
food. Instead, concentrate on slipping the spatula under
the food, folding over, and then tossing quickly.

Deep-frying Tips

Deep-frying in Chinese cooking usually involves batter-dipped pieces of meat or the frying of appetizers wrapped in a flour-based skin, such as egg rolls. Most deep-frying recipes involve two steps. The first step in deep-frying is to cook the items to a golden brown followed by draining. The next step involves heating the oil again and refrying. This ensures a crisp, evenly cooked end product and also makes entertaining a snap, as you can complete the first step of deep-frying the day before and refry when your guests arrive the following evening.

Deep-frying also requires very high heat levels (350°F.). Make sure the oil isn't too hot, because food will over-cook on the outside and will be undercooked on the inside. It isn't necessary to use a wok when deep-frying, but you must always use a deep pan to adequately cover the items you are frying. For example, if you are using 2 inches of oil, you must leave 6 inches of space above the oil. If your oil begins smoking, turn off the heat for a few minutes and let the oil return to 350°F. Heat oil uncovered to prevent over-heating.

Also, if the temperature is too low, then it will soak up too much oil. It's very important that anything you deep-fry is dried completely, especially before you dip items into batter or marinade. Vegetable and corn oil are preferred for deep-frying.

Steaming Tips

Steaming is the healthiest method in chinese cooking.
You can create a lower-fat alternative to certain recipes by
steaming. For example, almost any dumpling recipe can be
steamed rather than fried.

When steaming, make sure to bring water to a rolling boil
and maintain heat levels while cooking. You may use your
own stockpot to steam: simply use two cans (such as
empty tuna fish cans) to raise a platter 2 inches above the
water. When steaming dumplings, you may use sliced carrots under the dumplings to prevent them from sticking.
It's important to ensure there is enough water so it doesn't
evaporate and leave you with a scorched pot. Whether you
use a wok, stockpot, or traditional steamer, make sure
items are raised above the water and that you use a
secure lid.

Smoking Tips

It's very easy to re-create the flavor of authentic smoked Chinese dishes in your own kitchen. This method provides a glaze created by the smoking of brown sugar, black tea, and raw rice.

When smoking, make sure to line a pan with foil or else the brown sugar will ruin the pan. You can use any type of heavy baking pan with the exception of a nonstick. Nonstick baking pans will not allow for high enough heat levels to achieve the desired smoking technique.

shredding (carrots)

Cut carrots in 2 x $\frac{1}{8}$-inch slices. Pile together and cut lengthwise into matchsticks.

dicing (tofu and zucchini)

The goal in dicing is to achieve a uniform, square shape. Cut into $1\frac{1}{2}$-inch slices and then into $1\frac{1}{2}$-inch strips. Cut across strips into $1\frac{1}{2}$-inch squares.

slicing (beef)

Cut beef into 2-inch-wide pieces with the grain. Slice against the grain into $\frac{1}{8}$-inch slices. For tender cuts of beef like tenderloin, you may simply cut into bite-size cubes.

cubing (zucchini and chicken)

Cut lengthwise into 1-inch strips. Cut across strips into $\frac{3}{4}$-inch cubes.

Starting with the corner closest to you, fold the end on top of the lettuce. Fold the sides in, then roll up.

Repeat the procedure with the remaining ingredients. Cut each roll in half diagonally, place on a chilled platter, and serve with the chilled dipping sauce.

chicken skewers

makes 12 skewers

It's easy to overcook chicken, so keep your eye on the skewers. You can marinate the chicken in the refrigerator all day until you're ready to cook them that night. Cut up leftover chicken and toss with mixed greens for lunch the next day.

12	(6-inch) wooden skewers	1	teaspoon cornstarch
1	pound skinless, boneless chicken breast	1	teaspoon salt
		1	teaspoon dark soy sauce
marinade		½	teaspoon sugar
1	tablespoon vegetable oil	¼	teaspoon white pepper
2	teaspoons dry white wine	¼	teaspoon sesame oil
1	teaspoon finely chopped fresh ginger		

Soak the wooden skewers in water for 30 minutes.

Cut the chicken into 2 × ½-inch strips. In a glass or plastic bowl, mix the vegetable oil, wine, ginger, cornstarch, salt, soy sauce, sugar, pepper, and sesame oil. Add the chicken and stir.

Cover and refrigerate for 30 minutes.

Preheat the broiler.

Thread 3 chicken strips onto each skewer. Repeat the procedure until all the skewers are prepared.

Broil about 4 inches from the heat, turning once, until done, about 5 minutes.

crispy shrimp wrapped in bacon

makes about 20 pieces

This recipe can be made ahead and reheated in a hot oven or briefly refried. Keep a batch in the freezer for a colorful first course when unexpected company arrives.

1	pound large shrimp, in the shell (about 20)		20	strips bacon
1½	teaspoons salt, divided		¼	cup all-purpose flour
1	large egg white		2	tablespoons cornstarch
½	teaspoon minced garlic		¼	teaspoon baking soda
	Pinch white pepper		5	cups vegetable oil, divided
20	strips carrot			

Remove the shells from the shrimp, leaving the tails intact. Devein the shrimp. Place warm water in a bowl and add 1 teaspoon salt; stir to dissolve. Place the shrimp in the salt water and swirl. Leave the shrimp in the salt water for 5 minutes, then rinse with cold water and drain. Pat dry on paper towels. Mix the shrimp with the egg white, ¼ teaspoon salt, the garlic, and pepper.

Place 1 carrot strip on top of the shrimp. Wrap the bacon strip around the shrimp and carrot.

To make the batter, in a bowl, combine the flour, cornstarch, baking soda, ¼ cup water, ½ tablespoon oil, and the remaining ¼ teaspoon salt and mix well. Brush the shrimp with batter until well coated.

In a deep-frying pan, heat the remaining oil to 350°F. Fry 6 wrapped shrimp at a time until light brown, turning occasionally, for 3 to 4 minutes. Drain on paper towels. Repeat with the remaining shrimp. Increase the oil temperature to 375°F. Fry the shrimp again all at one time until golden brown, about 1 minute. Drain on paper towels and serve hot.

fish cakes

The combination of fish and tofu makes this appetizer high in protein and gives it a unique firm texture. They keep in the freezer up to 4 to 5 weeks for a quick lunch or you may add them to soup.

4 ounces long green beans	2 tablespoons cornstarch
1¼ teaspoons salt, divided	1 teaspoon sesame oil
½ pound shrimp, deveined	¼ teaspoon white pepper
½ pound skinless fish fillets (salmon, walleye, sea bass)	1 large egg
1 teaspoon finely chopped fresh ginger	2 tablespoons + 1 teaspoon vegetable oil, divided
10 ounces firm tofu	1 teaspoon minced garlic
¼ cup chopped cilantro leaves	½ cup all-purpose flour

Wash and drain the green beans. Dice into ¼-inch pieces.

Place warm water in a bowl and add 1 teaspoon salt; stir to dissolve. Place the shrimp in the salt water and swirl. Leave the shrimp in the salt water for 5 minutes, then rinse with cold water and drain. Pat dry on paper towels. Finely chop the shrimp into a paste (you may use a food processor). Rinse the fish with cold water and pat dry. Finely chop the fish into a paste. Combine with the shrimp paste and add the ginger and ⅛ teaspoon salt. In a medium bowl, mash the tofu with a fork. Stir in the shrimp/fish paste, cilantro, cornstarch, sesame oil, pepper, and egg with a fork until well mixed. Set aside.

Heat a skillet over high heat and add 1 teaspoon vegetable oil. Stir-fry the garlic, green beans, and the remaining ⅛ teaspoon salt until the beans turn bright green, about 1 minute. Remove from the pan, spreading the beans out to cool. When the green beans have cooled, add to the shrimp/fish mixture. Divide the mixture into 8 parts and form into patties. Dip each patty into flour to coat.

Heat a large nonstick skillet over medium heat and add the remaining 2 tablespoons oil. Over high heat, fry the fish cakes for 1 minute, then turn over and fry for 1 minute, or until both sides are golden brown. If the fish cakes are browning too quickly, reduce the heat. Add oil as needed if the fish cakes stick to the pan. Remove from the skillet and place on a heated platter.

garlic chicken wings

Make sure the chicken marinates for at least 30 minutes and up to 12 hours to ensure the proper flavor. Buy precut chicken wings for ease of preparation.

12	chicken wings	1	teaspoon minced garlic
1	tablespoon vegetable oil	1	teaspoon minced fresh ginger
2	teaspoons soy sauce	½	teaspoon salt
¼	cup ketchup	1	tablespoon sugar

Cut the chicken wings at the joints to make 3 pieces. Reserve the tip thirds to use in broth.

In a small bowl, mix the vegetable oil, soy sauce, ketchup, garlic, ginger, salt, and sugar together. Pour over the wings and marinate 1 to 2 hours in the refrigerator.

Preheat the oven to 400°F.

Bake for 40 minutes in a shallow roasting pan (line it with foil for easy cleaning). Stir 3 to 4 times while baking.

honey-glazed spareribs

You may substitute ³/₄ cup sugar for the honey. The ribs can be made ahead and are just as delicious served the next day, reheated or served cold.

2	pounds pork back ribs, cut lengthwise across bones into halves	1	cup Chicken Broth (page 52)
1	large egg	¾	cup white vinegar
3	teaspoons salt, divided	3	cups vegetable oil, divided
2	teaspoons soy sauce, divided	1	minced garlic clove
½	cup + ½ teaspoon sugar, divided	1	tablespoon hot pepper sauce
½	teaspoon five-spice powder	6	tablespoons cornstarch, divided
¾	cup honey	¾	cup all-purpose flour
		½	teaspoon baking soda

Trim the fat and remove the membrane from the ribs. Cut between each rib to separate. In a glass or plastic bowl, mix the egg, 1 teaspoon salt, 1 teaspoon soy sauce, ½ cup sugar, and the five-spice powder; stir in the ribs. Cover and refrigerate 30 minutes or longer. Drain the ribs, reserving the marinade.

To make the sauce, in a 3-quart saucepan, heat the remaining ½ teaspoon sugar, the honey, chicken broth, vinegar, 1 tablespoon vegetable oil, the remaining 1 teaspoon soy sauce, 1 teaspoon salt, the garlic, and hot pepper sauce to boiling. Mix 4 tablespoons cornstarch with ¼ cup cold water and stir into the sauce. Cook and stir until thickened, about 20 seconds. Set aside.

Heat the remaining vegetable oil (about 1½ inches deep) in a wok to 350°F. To make the batter, add enough water to the reserved marinade to measure ¾ cup. Mix with the flour, the remaining 2 tablespoons cornstarch, the remaining 1 teaspoon salt, and the baking soda. Stir the ribs into the batter until well coated. Fry 10 to 12 ribs at a time until light brown, turning occasionally, for 3 to 4 minutes. Drain on paper towels. Increase the oil temperature to 375°F. Fry the ribs again until golden brown, about 1 minute. Drain on paper towels.

Reheat the sauce and pour over the ribs.

lettuce cups with turkey

If you prepare the turkey mixture ahead, you can create this appetizer in 5 minutes as guests arrive. Toss leftover cooked meat mixture with noodles for a delicious and simple lunch the next day. You may substitute ground chicken or pork.

1	pound turkey breast	2	teaspoons vegetable oil
½	teaspoon salt	½	cup coarsely chopped water chestnuts
¼	teaspoon sugar	3	large shallots, peeled and chopped
¼	teaspoon white pepper	2	ounces diced pimiento
2	teaspoons cornstarch	½	cup hoisin sauce
1	small head iceberg or Bibb lettuce	1	chopped green onion

Remove and discard the tendon from the turkey; dry the turkey breast with paper towels. Dice the turkey into ½-inch pieces.

In a medium bowl, combine the salt, sugar, pepper, and cornstarch. Add the turkey, cover, and refrigerate for 20 minutes.

Carefully remove the lettuce leaves from the head. Take the 6 largest, nicest bowl-shaped leaves. Reserve the remaining leaves for another use. Trim the edges to form a 4-inch bowl.

Heat a large, deep nonstick skillet with a high edge over high heat. Add the vegetable oil, turkey, water chestnuts, and shallots. Using 2 spoons, stir and separate until the turkey turns white, about 2 minutes. Add the pimiento and stir-fry for 1 minute. Remove from the heat.

Brush approximately 1 teaspoon hoisin sauce, or to taste, on each lettuce leaf. Place ⅓ cup filling in the center of each lettuce leaf, garnish with green onion, and serve with the remaining hoisin sauce.

panfried pork dumplings

Children love dumplings and this recipe is a favorite in our family. Keep uncooked dumplings in the freezer on hand for steaming, boiling, or frying. They are also great in soup. You may use ground chicken in place of the pork.

8	ounces celery cabbage (Napa cabbage)			Dash white pepper
3	teaspoons salt, divided		2	cups all-purpose flour
1	pound lean ground pork		2	to 4 tablespoons vegetable oil
¼	cup finely chopped green onions, with tops			
1	tablespoon white wine			

dipping sauce

1	teaspoon cornstarch		¼	cup soy sauce
1	teaspoon sesame oil		1	teaspoon sesame oil

Cut the celery cabbage across into thin strips. Mix with 2 teaspoons salt and set aside for 5 minutes. Squeeze out the excess moisture.

In a large bowl, mix the celery cabbage, pork, green onions, wine, cornstarch, the remaining 1 teaspoon salt, 1 teaspoon sesame oil, and the pepper.

In a bowl, mix the flour and 1 cup boiling water until a soft dough forms. Knead the dough on a lightly floured surface about 5 minutes, or until smooth.

Divide the dough in half. Shape each half into a roll 12 inches long and cut each roll into ½-inch slices.

Roll 1 slice of dough into a 3-inch circle and place 1 tablespoon pork mixture in the center of the circle. Lift up the edges of the circle and pinch 5 pleats up to create a pouch to encase the mixture. Pinch the top together. Repeat with the remaining slices of dough and filling.

Heat a wok or nonstick skillet until very hot. Add 1 tablespoon vegetable oil, tilting the wok to coat the sides. If using a nonstick skillet, add ½ tablespoon vegetable oil. Place 12 dumplings in a single layer in the wok and fry 2 minutes, or until the bottoms are golden brown.

Add ½ cup water. Cover and cook 6 to 7 minutes, or until the water is absorbed. Repeat with the remaining dumplings.

To make a dipping sauce, in a small bowl, mix the soy sauce with 1 teaspoon sesame oil. Serve with the dumplings.

firecracker shrimp

This festive appetizer, which is great for a Fourth of July gathering or Chinese New Year celebration, looks just like a firecracker. In China, firecrackers light up the sky on New Year's Day. Prepare it a day ahead and save the frying step for just after your guests arrive.

12	large shrimp, in the shell
1	teaspoon salt
½	teaspoon garlic salt, divided
4	sheets spring roll wrappers
24	carrot strips (3 × ¼ inch)
1	egg, beaten

dipping sauce

¼	cup mayonnaise
2	tablespoons hot pepper sauce
3	cups vegetable oil for deep-frying

Removing the shells and leaving the tail intact, make a deep cut lengthwise down the back of each shrimp; wash out the sand vein. Place warm water in a bowl and add the salt; stir to dissolve. Place the shrimp in the salt water and swirl. Leave the shrimp in the salt water for 5 minutes, then rinse with cold water, drain, and pat dry on paper towels. Sprinkle with ¼ teaspoon garlic salt.

Cut each spring roll wrapper into thirds, making 3 long narrow strips.

Place the carrot strips in a small bowl, sprinkle with the remaining ¼ teaspoon garlic salt, and set aside.

Brush the egg at the top of the shrimp. Place 2 carrot strips in the slit of each shrimp. Brush each spring roll strip with egg and roll each shrimp up tightly in the spring roll strip, with the egg holding it together. The tail of the shrimp should be protruding from one end and the carrots from the other—to resemble a firecracker! Continue the process until all the wrappers are rolled with the shrimp and carrots.

To make a dipping sauce, in a small bowl, mix the mayonnaise and hot pepper sauce. Set aside.

In a wok, heat the vegetable oil to 350°F. Fry the shrimp rolls until golden brown, about 2 minutes, turning 2 to 3 times. Drain on paper towels. Serve with the dipping sauce.

siu mai

This is a traditional dumpling recipe, served open faced, and commonly found as part of dim sum (Chinese brunch). You may use pork instead of chicken, if you wish. If you cannot find siu mai wrappers, use egg roll wrappers cut into fourths, then cut the corners off to form a more circular shape.

4 medium dried black mushrooms	1 teaspoon finely chopped fresh ginger
1½ teaspoons salt, divided	2 tablespoons finely chopped carrot
½ pound medium shrimp, peeled and deveined	4 tablespoons finely chopped onion
10 ounces skinless, boneless chicken breast	**dipping sauce**
⅛ teaspoon white pepper	3 tablespoons light soy sauce
½ teaspoon sesame oil	½ teaspoon sugar
½ egg white	1 tablespoon chopped green onion, with tops
1 tablespoon cornstarch	
2 teaspoons vegetable oil	18 siu mai wrappers

Soak the mushrooms in hot water for 15 to 20 minutes, or until soft. Rinse them in cold water and drain. Squeeze out any excess water. Remove and discard the stems and cut the mushrooms into ¼-inch pieces.

Pour 2 cups warm water in a bowl. Add 1 teaspoon salt and stir to dissolve. Place the shrimp in the salt water and swirl. Leave the shrimp in the salt water for 5 minutes, then rinse with cold water, drain, and pat dry with paper towels. Cut the shrimp into ¼-inch diced pieces.

Trim the excess fat from the chicken and cut into ¼-inch diced pieces. In a small bowl, to make the marinade, mix the pepper, sesame oil, egg white, cornstarch, vegetable oil, the remaining ½ teaspoon salt, the ginger, carrot, and onion. Add the chicken, shrimp, and mushrooms; mix very well and set aside.

To make a dipping sauce, in a small bowl, mix the soy sauce, sugar, 1 tablespoon water, and the chopped green onion.

Place 1 tablespoon of the chicken and shrimp mixture in the center of a siu mai wrapper and bring the edges up around the filling, leaving the top open. Repeat with the remaining siu mai wrappers.

Place the dumplings in a single layer on a rack in a steamer, cover, and steam over boiling water for 12 minutes. (Add boiling water if necessary.)

spicy beef skewers

makes 12 skewers

Marinate the beef in the refrigerator up to 24 hours in advance. You can cook these crowd-pleasing appetizers under the broiler or on an outdoor grill. Serve with Chicken (page 33) and Scallop Skewers (page 46) and create an Asian barbecue cocktail party.

12 (6-inch) wooden skewers
1 tablespoon baking soda
1½ pounds beef flank steak

marinade
2 tablespoons vegetable oil
1 teaspoon light soy sauce

1 teaspoon salt
1 tablespoon minced garlic
1 tablespoon finely minced fresh ginger
1 teaspoon sugar
1 teaspoon cayenne
2 tablespoons cornstarch
¼ cup hoisin sauce

Soak the wooden skewers in water for 30 minutes.

In a large, flat pan, dissolve the baking soda in 2 cups water. Add the beef and soak for 10 minutes.

Remove the beef from the water and pat dry with paper towels. With a knife held at a sharp angle, cut across the grain into thin slices, about 2 × 5 inches long. Place the beef onto a large flat platter.

In a small bowl, to make the marinade, combine the vegetable oil, soy sauce, salt, garlic, ginger, sugar, cayenne, cornstarch, and hoisin sauce. Brush both sides of the beef with the marinade. Refrigerate for 30 minutes or longer.

Thread 2 beef strips onto a 6-inch skewer. Repeat the procedure to use the remaining skewers.

Preheat the broiler.

Broil with the tops of the meat about 4 inches from the heat for about 2 minutes. Turn the skewers and broil for 2 additional minutes.

steamed shrimp rolls

These excellent low-fat appetizers are perfect for a brunch gathering. Serve with a variety of dumplings and create an authentic dim sum get-together. You may substitute chopped green onions for cilantro.

1½ teaspoons salt, divided
1 pound medium shrimp, peeled and deveined
12 sheets rice paper wrappers
¼ cup canned and drained water chestnuts, minced
¼ teaspoon white pepper
1 large egg white
1 teaspoon sesame oil

1 teaspoon vegetable oil
1 tablespoon cornstarch
½ cup chopped cilantro leaves

dipping sauce

1 tablespoon hot chili sauce
¼ cup mayonnaise
1 tablespoon light soy sauce

Place 2 cups warm water in a bowl and add 1 teaspoon salt; stir to dissolve. Place the shrimp in the salt water and swirl. Leave the shrimp in the salt water for 5 minutes, then rinse with cold water, drain, and pat dry with paper towels. Using a food processor or a sharp knife, chop the shrimp into a paste.

Wet 2 large kitchen towels, wring them out, and lay them flat on the counter. Dip a wrapper in hot water and place on the wet towel. Dip another and place it next to the first. Cover the wrappers with another wet towel. Repeat the procedure, making sure the wrappers don't stack or they'll stick together. Allow the wrappers to sit for 5 minutes.

In a bowl, combine the shrimp and water chestnuts. Stir in the remaining ½ teaspoon salt, the pepper, egg white, sesame oil, vegetable oil, and cornstarch. Stir to mix very well.

Place 2 tablespoons shrimp mixture centered on the bottom of a rice paper wrapper. Sprinkle a teaspoon of chopped cilantro over the shrimp filling. Fold the bottom up, fold the sides in, and roll into a 3 × 2-inch roll. Repeat the procedure with the remaining wrappers. Place the finished rolls ½ inch apart in a single layer on a plate, using 2 plates if necessary.

In a small bowl, stir together the chili sauce, mayonnaise, and soy sauce. Set aside.

Place the plate containing the shrimp rolls on an oiled rack in a steamer. Cover and steam over boiling water 8 minutes, adding more boiling water if necessary.

Repeat with the remaining rolls. Serve with the dipping sauce.

thousand-corner
shrimp balls

You can prepare these ahead and fry them at the last minute. Popular and impressive, this appetizer can be served as a cocktail hors d'oeuvre or as part of a dim sum brunch. Keep a batch of these shrimp balls frozen and add to chicken stock for a quick soup, or have ready for a fast starter at your next party. Serve them with the dipping sauce on page 31.

2	teaspoons salt, divided	2	teaspoons vegetable oil
1	pound medium shrimp, peeled and deveined	1/8	teaspoon white pepper
4	ounces soft tofu	1	bag (1 pound) thinly sliced firm white bread, such as Pepperidge Farm
2	large egg whites	3	to 4 cups vegetable oil for deep-frying
2	tablespoons cornstarch		
1	teaspoon sesame oil		

Place warm water in a bowl and add 1 teaspoon salt; stir to dissolve. Place the shrimp in the salt water and swirl. Leave for 5 minutes, then rinse with cold water, drain, and pat dry with paper towels. Using a sharp knife or a food processor, chop the shrimp to a paste.

Mash the tofu with a fork in a bowl and add the shrimp, the remaining 1 teaspoon salt, the egg whites, cornstarch, sesame oil, 2 teaspoons vegetable oil, and the pepper. Mix well.

In a wok or large skillet, heat the vegetable oil to 350°F. Remove the crusts from the bread and cut into very tiny squares (about 1/16 inch). Spread the bread squares on a sheet pan, spoon 1 tablespoon shrimp mixture on the bread squares, and roll into a ball (the bread corners from the little squares should be protruding from the shrimp/tofu ball). Fry 6 balls at a time for 2 to 3 minutes, turning so they brown evenly. Let drain briefly on paper towels.

tofu and shrimp
medallions

serves 4

You can substitute crabmeat for the cooked shrimp. Freeze the cooked patties and you'll have them on hand to crumble into fried rice or panfry for a quick and nutritious lunch.

1½	teaspoons salt, divided		2	small egg whites
8	ounces shrimp, peeled and deveined		¼	teaspoon white pepper
2	tablespoons cornstarch		1	tablespoon vegetable oil
1	teaspoon sesame oil		1	teaspoon oyster sauce
14	ounces soft tofu			

Place 2 cups warm water in a bowl and add 1 teaspoon salt; stir to dissolve. Place the shrimp in the salt water and swirl. Leave the shrimp in the salt water for 5 minutes, then rinse with cold water, drain, and pat dry with paper towels. Dice the shrimp. In a small bowl, combine the diced shrimp with the cornstarch and sesame oil.

In a bowl, mash the tofu with a fork in a bowl and add the egg whites, remaining ½ teaspoon salt, and the pepper. Stir and mix well. Add to the shrimp mixture.

Preheat the oven to 450°F.

Brush a cookie sheet with the vegetable oil. Divide the tofu mixture into 8 equal parts, form into balls, and flatten into ½-inch patties on the cookie sheet. Bake in the oven for 8 minutes, turn over, and bake an additional 8 minutes, or until lightly brown.

Place on a platter, drizzle the medallions with the oyster sauce, and serve.

scallop skewers

Scallops should be fresh and moist when you buy them. Don't overcook them or they'll become tough. These skewers go well with a light salad as a healthy entrée.

20	(6-inch) wooden skewers
1	pound medium sea scallops (20 per pound)

marinade

2	teaspoons vegetable oil
½	teaspoon salt
2	teaspoons minced garlic
1	teaspoon cornstarch
1	tablespoon oyster sauce (optional)

Soak the wooden skewers in water for 30 minutes.

Taking each scallop in your hand, remove the small muscle on the side of the scallop. Rinse each scallop under cold water and gently pat dry. Lay each scallop flat on paper towels.

In a small bowl, combine the oil, salt, garlic, and cornstarch. Brush both sides of the scallops with the marinade.

Skewer a scallop slightly off center. Skewer the scallop again on the other side, again slightly off center, so the 2 skewers are parallel. Add another scallop to the same set of skewers, following the same procedure.

Preheat a grill to high heat and lightly brush the grill rack with oil. Place the scallops on the grill for approximately 1 minute. Turn the scallops and grill the other side for another minute. Lightly brush the scallops with additional vegetable oil if needed to prevent sticking. If desired, serve with oyster sauce.

scallops wrapped with bacon

serves 4

This rich, tasty, and filling appetizer can also be served as a main dish. Make sure the scallops are completely dry after you rinse them or they'll spatter oil.

10	large sea scallops (about 1 pound)
1	teaspoon vegetable oil
1	teaspoon garlic salt
1	tablespoon cornstarch
5	strips bacon, halved crosswise

dipping sauce

¼	teaspoon hoisin sauce
2	tablespoons balsamic vinegar

Remove the muscles on the side of the scallops, rinse with cold water, and pat dry with paper towels. Brush the scallops with vegetable oil and sprinkle with the garlic salt. Coat the scallops with cornstarch.

Wrap the half strips of bacon around the sides of the scallops. Use a toothpick to secure the ends of the bacon to the scallops. Repeat until all the scallops are wrapped.

In a small bowl, mix the hoisin sauce and balsamic vinegar together to make a dipping sauce.

Preheat the broiler and place the scallops on a broiler pan. Cook for 3 to 4 minutes and turn over. Cook 2 minutes longer, or until the bacon browns. Serve with the sauce.

sea legs wrapped in shrimp and tofu

serves 4

Fresh minced crabmeat makes a nice variation instead of shrimp.

1½ teaspoons salt, divided	4 ounces soft tofu
1 pound medium shrimp, peeled and deveined	½ teaspoon minced garlic
4 ounces canned water chestnuts, drained	2 tablespoons bread crumbs
1 shallot, peeled	2 tablespoons cornstarch
1 large egg white	4 ounces sea legs
½ teaspoon sugar	2 teaspoons vegetable oil
¼ teaspoon white pepper	¼ cup Chicken Broth (page 52)
1 tablespoon cornstarch	Light soy sauce

Place warm water in a bowl and add 1 teaspoon salt; stir to dissolve. Place the shrimp in the salt water and swirl. Leave the shrimp in the salt water for 5 minutes, then rinse with cold water and drain. Pat dry on paper towels.

In a food processor, finely chop the water chestnuts and shallot. Add the shrimp, egg white, the remaining ½ teaspoon salt, sugar, pepper, cornstarch, tofu, and garlic and process to chop finely.

In a small bowl, combine the bread crumbs and cornstarch. Evenly spread the mixture on a piece of wax paper.

Take ¼ cup filling and form into a 4 × 2-inch rectangle. Set on the bread crumb and cornstarch mixture.

Place 1 sea leg in the center of the mixture and wrap the mixture around the sea leg. Continue the process until finished.

Heat a large nonstick skillet over medium heat. Add the vegetable oil. Place the wrapped sea legs in the pan, not touching. Panfry the sea legs, continuously rolling them, until light brown, about 2 minutes.

Add the chicken broth. Continue to cook and roll until the sea legs are golden brown and the chicken broth is fully absorbed, about 5 minutes. Serve with light soy sauce.

vegetable dumplings

In northern China, dumplings are often served for lunch or dinner. When you have guests for brunch, these are good served with Firecracker Shrimp (page 40) and Siu Mai (page 41). They can be prepared ahead of time. It will take 1 minute (or until hot) to reheat 20 dumplings in the microwave, or you can reheat them in a frying pan in 2 tablespoons of water over medium heat for 3 to 5 minutes, covered.

1	pound wonton or siu mai wrappers
1	ounce dried black mushrooms
2	ounces canned Sichuan preserved cabbage
4	ounces fresh peas
4	ounces chopped green onion, white part only
4	ounces chopped carrot
1	teaspoon sesame oil
	Pinch sugar

1	small egg white
2	tablespoons vegetable oil, divided

dipping sauce

2	tablespoons soy sauce
1	tablespoon balsamic vinegar
½	teaspoon minced garlic

If the wonton wrappers are square, trim them into circles and cover with a damp towel. Set aside.

Soak the black mushrooms in hot water for 20 minutes, or until soft. Rinse with cold water a few times, squeezing out the excess water. Cut off and discard the stems. In a food processor or by hand, coarsely chop the mushroom caps. Place in a medium bowl. Rinse the Sichuan cabbage in cold water and pat dry with paper towels. Coarsely chop into small diced pieces. Add to the mushrooms. Add the peas, green onion, carrot, sesame oil, and sugar and mix together for the filling.

Beat the egg white with 1 tablespoon water for sealing the dumplings.

Place 2 teaspoons filling in the center of each wonton circle. Brush with the egg mixture along the edge and fold over to form a half circle.

Heat a large, nonstick skillet over high heat. Add 1 tablespoon vegetable oil and reduce the heat to medium.

Add 20 dumplings and panfry for 1 minute. Add ½ cup water, cover, and cook 1 minute. Remove the cover and continue to cook until the water is fully absorbed, about 2 minutes. Repeat the process until all the dumplings are cooked.

In a small bowl, blend the soy sauce, vinegar, and garlic and serve as a dipping sauce with the hot dumplings.

soups

Beef Broth

Chicken Broth

Fish Broth

Vegetable Broth

Beef with Rice Stick Noodle Soup

Chicken, Bok Choy, and Clam Soup

Coconut Chicken Soup

Fish and Tomato Soup

Fish and Watercress Soup

Hunan Beef Noodle Soup

Miso Soup with Clams

Peanut Soup

Sea Bass and Tomato Soup

Seafood Hot-and-Sour Soup

Shredded Pork with Soybean Sprouts Soup

Spicy Pork Noodle Soup

Sun-Dried Scallops, Tofu, and Spinach Soup

Tofu Tomato Soup

Tomato Beef Egg Drop Soup

Velvet Beef Cilantro Soup

Velvet Chicken Corn Soup

beef broth

This broth is a staple for sauces and soups. Freeze leftover beef bones to make into stock.

1	pound beef shanks	1	small onion, sliced
2	pounds meaty beef bones	8	cups boiling water
2	teaspoons vegetable oil	1	teaspoon salt
4	(¼-inch) slices fresh ginger	¼	teaspoon white pepper

Rinse the beef shanks and bones with cold water and pat dry with paper towels. Heat a large stockpot over high heat and add the vegetable oil, ginger, onion, beef shanks, and bones. Stir-fry 3 minutes to brown, turning 2 to 3 times. Add the boiling water. Cook, uncovered, for 10 minutes over high heat. Reduce the heat to low and cover partially. Simmer gently for 3 hours.

Remove the broth from the heat and let cool. Strain the broth through a strainer into a bowl and let stand until the fat rises to the surface. Using a large spoon, skim off the fat, add the salt and pepper, and stir to blend. When the broth is cool, refrigerate in a clear container for up to 5 days. The broth may also be frozen up to 6 months.

chicken broth

makes 8 cups

This is a staple in virtually all stir-fry dishes and soups. Freeze small 2-tablespoon portions in ice cube trays for convenience when stir-frying.

3   pounds chicken, cut up   4   (¼-inch) slices fresh ginger

Rinse the chicken in cold water. Remove any visible fat. Cut away the breast meat and save it for another use. In a large soup pot, place 8 cups water and bring to a boil. Add the chicken, including the breast bones and gizzards, and the ginger. Return to a boil and cook 5 minutes over high heat. Reduce the heat to low, cover, and simmer for 2 hours.

Strain the broth and let cool to room temperature. Skim off any visible fat. Refrigerate in a clear container for up to 5 days. The broth may also be frozen for up to 6 months.

fish broth

Fish broth, the base for seafood soups, is very healthy and is used in many sauces. Freeze leftover fish bones to make stock, and keep frozen fish broth on hand for quick soups.

2	pounds snapper bones and head	2	teaspoons finely chopped fresh ginger
1	leek, white part only	2	teaspoons minced garlic
2	tablespoons vegetable oil	8	cups boiling water
2	chopped shallots	1	teaspoon salt

Clean the bones and head. Cut the fish head into 4 to 6 pieces. Make sure to remove all traces of blood. Remove the gills and rinse the fish thoroughly under cold water.

Cut the leek in half lengthwise. Wash very well to remove the sand; dry with paper towels. Cut into ½-inch slices across the leek stalk.

Heat a large stockpot and add the vegetable oil. Stir-fry the leek, shallots, ginger, and garlic for 1 minute. Add the bones, boiling water, and salt and cook for 2 minutes over high heat. Lower the heat and cook, partially covered, for 40 minutes. After the broth is done, strain through cheesecloth or a fine-mesh strainer to remove all the bones and vegetables. Cool, then refrigerate or freeze in tightly sealed containers.

vegetable broth

A staple in vegetarian dishes, this stock may be frozen for future use to make a variety of soups.

4	leeks, white part only	1	carrot, peeled and sliced
1	ounce dried black mushrooms	1	teaspoon salt
1	tablespoon vegetable oil	⅛	teaspoon white pepper
10	ounces soybean sprouts		

Remove and discard the tough outer layers of the leeks. Cut the leeks open and in half lengthwise. Wash very well to remove any sand; dry with paper towels. Cut into 1-inch pieces across the leek stalks.

Soak the mushrooms in hot water for 20 minutes, or until soft; drain. Rinse in warm water; drain. Squeeze out any excess moisture. Remove and discard the stems.

Heat a large stockpot and add the vegetable oil. Add the leeks and stir-fry for 1 minute. Add 4 cups water, bring to a boil, and add the black mushrooms, soybean sprouts, carrot, salt, and pepper. Return to boiling again, turn the heat down to medium-low, and cook, covered, for 1 hour. Strain. Cool and store in the refrigerator for up to 5 days or freeze in a tightly sealed container for up to 3 months.

beef with rice stick noodle soup

serves 2 to 3

Large grocery stores carry rice sticks in the Asian section. You may use any other type of noodle in this dish, although you'll need to follow the package directions so that the noodles are fully cooked first. Use your best-quality broth to ensure a rich and flavorful soup.

5	ounces dried rice stick noodles		4	cups Chicken Broth (page 52) or Beef Broth (page 51)
4	ounces beef sirloin or flank steak		1	tablespoon fish sauce
¼	teaspoon salt		½	teaspoon sesame oil
⅛	teaspoon white pepper		2	tablespoons chopped cilantro leaves
1	teaspoon finely chopped fresh ginger			
½	teaspoon cornstarch			

Soak the dried rice noodles in warm water for 15 minutes; drain. Rinse with cold water and set aside.

Cut the beef into thin slices. In a bowl, mix with the salt, pepper, ginger, and cornstarch. Set aside.

In a large soup pot, bring 6 cups water to a boil. Add the noodles and boil for 30 seconds. Drain well and place the noodles in serving bowls.

Put the broth in a 3-quart soup pot. Bring to a boil. Stir in the beef, fish sauce, and sesame oil, return to boiling, and cook for 20 seconds. Turn off the heat. Pour the beef soup over the noodles and garnish with the cilantro leaves.

chicken, bok choy, and clam soup

serves 4

This soup is great for company. Take chicken broth out of the freezer and simply add bok choy and clams or try shrimp or scallops.

1	pound whole chicken breast	1	tablespoon vegetable oil
16	clams	2	teaspoons minced garlic
1	teaspoon salt	¼	cup red wine
2	thin slices fresh ginger	1	green onion, minced
2	cups sliced bok choy		

Rinse the chicken with cold water and set aside.

Brush the clams very well under cold running water; drain well.

In a medium saucepan, boil 5 cups water with the salt and ginger. Add the chicken breast and return to boiling. Reduce the heat and simmer for 10 minutes. Turn off the heat and let sit, covered, for 15 minutes. Remove the chicken from the liquid and remove the skin and bones from the chicken. Slice the chicken into ¼-inch strips across the meat; set aside.

Return the broth to boiling and add the bones from the chicken breast. Cook over medium heat, partially covered, for 30 minutes. Remove the bones from the soup and add the bok choy. Boil for 1 minute.

In a saucepan, while the stock is simmering, heat the vegetable oil. Add the garlic and clams and cook for 30 seconds. Add the red wine, cover, and cook for 2 minutes, or until all the clams are open (discard any clams that stay closed). Remove the clams and pour the clam cooking liquid into the soup. Bring the soup back to boiling. Turn off the heat. Pour into 4 serving bowls, place the chicken strips and 4 clams on top of each soup bowl, and garnish with the green onion.

coconut chicken soup

This is a very rich soup that is good followed by a light, stir-fry entrée. Fish sauce can be found at large grocery stores or Asian markets. You can freeze this soup or hold it in the refrigerator for a couple of days. Simply reheat on the stove or in a microwave and garnish with the cilantro. Shrimp can be used in place of the chicken.

6	ounces skinless, boneless chicken breast		2	teaspoons sugar
¼	teaspoon salt		1	tablespoon finely chopped fresh ginger
	Pinch white pepper		3	small fresh red chili peppers, seeded and thinly sliced
½	teaspoon cornstarch			
3	cups Chicken Broth (page 52)		¾	cup drained canned straw mushrooms
2	cups unsweetened coconut milk		¾	cup drained canned sliced bamboo shoots
3	tablespoons fresh lime juice		2	tablespoons coarsely chopped cilantro leaves
3	tablespoons fish sauce			

Cut the chicken breast into thin slices. In a bowl, mix the chicken breast slices with salt, pepper, and cornstarch; set aside.

In a 3-quart saucepan, combine the chicken broth, coconut milk, lime juice, fish sauce, sugar, ginger, chili peppers, straw mushrooms, and bamboo shoots and bring to a boil. When boiling, add the chicken breast slices. Stir to separate and return to a boil. When the chicken turns white, remove from the heat.

Place the soup in bowls and garnish with chopped cilantro leaves. Serve hot.

fish and tomato soup

Try this healthy and fast soup with shrimp or scallops if you prefer. Use fresh tomatoes from your garden for a fabulous summer treat.

6	ounces skinless fresh fish fillets, such as sea bass, walleye, or orange roughy	½	teaspoon sesame oil
⅛	teaspoon salt	1	teaspoon cornstarch
⅛	teaspoon white pepper	2	tomatoes
1	teaspoon finely chopped fresh ginger	4	cups Chicken Broth (page 52) or Fish Broth (page 53)
1	teaspoon vegetable oil	1	tablespoon chopped green onion

Rinse the fish with cold water and pat dry with paper towels. Cut into thin slices. In a bowl large enough to hold the fish, blend the salt, pepper, ginger, vegetable oil, sesame oil, and cornstarch. Add the fish and marinate for ½ hour or longer in the refrigerator.

Wash the tomatoes and cut into ½-inch wedges.

In a 3-quart saucepan, place the chicken broth and bring to a boil. Add the tomatoes and bring back to a boil. Add the fish slices, separating them carefully so as not to break into pieces. Bring the soup back to a boil and turn off the heat. Pour into a serving bowl and garnish with the green onion.

fish and watercress soup

Try spinach in this soup instead of watercress, and feel free to add other vegetables as well if you like.

6	ounces skinless fresh fish fillets, such as sea bass, halibut, walleye, or orange roughy	½	teaspoon sesame oil
¼	teaspoon salt, plus more to taste	8	ounces watercress
⅛	teaspoon white pepper	4	cups Chicken Broth (page 52) or Fish Broth (page 53)
1	teaspoon cornstarch	1	tablespoon chopped green onion
1	teaspoon finely chopped fresh ginger		

Rinse the fish fillets in cold water and pat dry. Cut into thin slices. In a bowl large enough to hold the fish, mix together the salt, pepper, cornstarch, ginger, and sesame oil. Add the fish, stir, and set aside.

Place the watercress in a large pot of cold water. Break off the tough ends of the watercress, wash well, and break the watercress into small pieces. Drain before using.

In a 3- or 4-quart saucepan, place the broth, bring to a boil, and add the watercress. Cook over high heat to boiling for 3 minutes. Add the fish slices. Return the soup to boiling and stir the fish gently to separate the pieces. Add salt to taste, place in serving bowls, and garnish with the green onion.

hunan beef noodle soup

The Hunan province is known for its abundance of red peppers. To make this soup spicier, add more chili peppers. This hearty soup can be served for lunch or as a light dinner. When cooking any noodle soup, remember that fresh noodles cook to double their uncooked weight and dried noodles cook to triple their uncooked weight. Fresh noodles may be found in most Asian markets.

4	ounces beef sirloin	2	tablespoons brown bean paste
¼	teaspoon salt	2	teaspoons minced garlic
¼	teaspoon white pepper	1	teaspoon finely chopped fresh ginger
1	teaspoon cornstarch	1	fresh red chili pepper, seeded and minced
6	ounces dried wide rice noodles or 10 ounces fresh wide rice noodles	4	cups Beef Broth (page 51) or Chicken Broth (page 52)
2	teaspoons vegetable oil	2	green onions, shredded, with tops

Cut the beef into 2 × ¼-inch thin slices. In a small bowl, mix together the salt, pepper, and cornstarch. Add the beef and marinate for 20 minutes.

In a bowl, soak the dried rice noodles in warm tap water for 15 minutes; drain. Rinse well with cold water. Drain well and set aside.

Heat a 3-quart saucepan over medium heat and add the vegetable oil. Add the brown bean paste, garlic, ginger, and chili pepper and sauté for 1 minute. Add the beef broth and bring to a boil. Add the noodles and return to boiling. Add the marinated beef and stir to separate the pieces. Return to boiling and turn off the heat. Pour into a serving bowl and garnish with the green onions.

miso soup with clams

Miso is a Japanese style of bean paste that can be found at Asian markets. Chinese bean paste can be used instead, but use a bit less, as it is more pungent.

20	Manila clams, unbroken and not open	3	tablespoons miso paste
4	cups Chicken Broth (page 52) or Fish Broth (page 53)	1	tablespoon finely chopped green onion
1	tablespoon white wine	¼	teaspoon sesame oil

Brush the clams very well under running cold water.

In a saucepan, place the chicken or fish broth and white wine and bring to a boil. Add the clams and return to a full boil, or until the clams open, about 3 minutes (discard any clams that do not open). Remove from the heat and stir in the miso. Pour into a serving bowl, garnish with the green onion, and sprinkle the sesame oil over the soup. Serve hot.

peanut soup

This vegetarian soup can be made ahead and frozen, then reheated in the microwave or on the stove. You may add pork bones for a richer soup unless you prefer a strict vegetarian preparation.

1	ounce dried black mushrooms		1	teaspoon minced garlic
1	cup peeled cubed potatoes		½	teaspoon cumin
1	cup peeled cubed carrots		¼	teaspoon cayenne
¾	cup raw skinless peanuts		2	medium tomatoes, cubed
1	teaspoon salt		2	tablespoons lime juice
1	tablespoon vegetable oil		2	teaspoons lemon juice
1	medium white onion, chopped		¼	cup miso paste

Soak the black mushrooms in hot water for 15 minutes, or until soft. Cut off and discard the stems. Cut the mushrooms into ½-inch diced pieces.

In a large soup pot, bring 6 cups water, the potatoes, carrots, peanuts, salt, and black mushrooms to a boil. Turn the heat down to medium-low, cover, and cook for 1 hour.

Heat a small skillet over high heat and add the vegetable oil. When hot, add the onion and garlic and sauté for 30 seconds. Add the cumin, cayenne, and tomatoes and sauté for 1 minute. Add to the soup. Return the soup to a boil for 10 minutes. Add the lime and lemon juices and the miso, stirring until the miso is dissolved. Turn off the heat and serve.

sea bass and tomato soup

You may also use walleye or orange roughy in this soup. Add other vegetables from your refrigerator or garden.

6	ounces skinless sea bass fillets	1	small red or green chili pepper, seeded and minced
¼	teaspoon sesame oil		
¼	teaspoon salt	1	cup thinly sliced celery
1	teaspoon finely chopped fresh ginger	4	cups Fish Broth (page 53) or Chicken Broth (page 52)
¼	teaspoon white pepper		
1	teaspoon cornstarch	½	cup cubed pineapple
2	small tomatoes	2	tablespoons fish sauce
2	teaspoons vegetable oil	2	tablespoons lime juice
2	teaspoons turmeric	¼	cup chopped fresh dill weed

Cut the sea bass into 1-inch cubes. In a bowl large enough to hold the fish, mix together the sesame oil, salt, ginger, pepper, and cornstarch. Add the sea bass cubes and toss to blend. Set aside.

Place the tomatoes in boiling water for 20 seconds. Remove the skin, cut into ¾-inch wedges, and cut each wedge in half.

In a 3-quart soup pot over medium heat, heat the vegetable oil. Add the tomatoes, turmeric, chili pepper, and celery and stir-fry for 1 minute. Add the broth, turn the heat up to high, and bring to a boil. Add the pineapple, fish sauce, and lime juice and boil for 1 minute, then add the fish cubes and dill. Bring back to a boil and boil briefly. Remove from the heat and serve.

seafood
hot-and-sour soup

serves 4

Use any leftover seafood or just shrimp for this flavorful soup. Add more white pepper for a spicier version. This recipe is great to make on weekends and can be reheated during the week.

1	tablespoon soy sauce		4	ounces drained canned shredded bamboo shoots
2	tablespoons cornstarch		2	large eggs, slightly beaten
½	teaspoon white pepper		4	ounces cooked shrimp
¼	teaspoon sugar		2	ounces cooked crabmeat or shredded sea legs
3	dried black mushrooms		1	tablespoon red pepper sauce
4	ounces firm tofu		½	teaspoon sesame oil
4	cups Chicken Broth (page 52) or Fish Broth (page 53)		1	green onion, with tops, diced
3	tablespoons white vinegar			

In a small bowl, combine the soy sauce, cornstarch, 2 tablespoons water, pepper, and sugar. Soak the black mushrooms in hot water for 20 minutes, or until soft. Rinse with cold water, then drain, squeezing out any excess moisture. Remove and discard the stems; cut the caps into thin strips. Cut the tofu into 2 × ¼-inch strips.

In a saucepan, heat the broth and vinegar to boiling. Add the bamboo shoots, black mushrooms, and tofu and return to a boil. Stir in the cornstarch mixture and bring to a rolling boil. Pour the beaten eggs slowly into the broth, stirring constantly with a fork until the eggs form threads. Add the shrimp, crabmeat, red pepper sauce, and sesame oil and stir. Return to a boil and boil for 20 seconds; turn off the heat. Pour into a serving bowl and garnish with the green onion.

shredded pork with soybean sprouts soup

Soybean sprouts can be found at Asian or specialty markets. They provide a sweet taste and crunchy texture to this soup. You may substitute shredded chicken if you wish.

4	ounces pork loin		1	teaspoon vegetable oil
	Dash salt		1	teaspoon finely chopped fresh ginger
	Dash white pepper		8	ounces soybean sprouts
½	teaspoon cornstarch		4	cups Chicken Broth (page 52)
1	small tomato			

Cut the pork into thin strips. In a small bowl, mix together the salt, pepper, and cornstarch and sprinkle over the pork. Toss and let sit for 15 minutes.

Place the tomato in boiling water for 2 minutes, peel the skin off the tomato, and cut into ½-inch wedges.

Heat a 3-quart saucepan over high heat and add the vegetable oil. When hot, add the ginger, soybean sprouts, and tomato. Stir-fry for about 1 minute. Add the chicken broth and bring to a boil. Continue cooking for 5 minutes. Stir in the pork and bring back to boiling; cook for 1 minute. Turn off the heat and serve.

spicy pork noodle soup

You can substitute beef or shrimp for the pork. If you keep dry noodles and chicken broth in your pantry, it is easy to make this recipe. If you have rich chicken broth you can eliminate the meat in this dish. You may also add any kind of vegetable; just return the broth to a boil and cook for 1 minute, before adding the noodles.

4	ounces pork tenderloin	2	green onions, with tops
¼	teaspoon salt	2	teaspoons vegetable oil
¼	teaspoon white pepper	2	tablespoons chili paste
1	teaspoon cornstarch	1	teaspoon minced garlic
6	ounces dried rice noodles (see Note)	4	cups Chicken Broth (page 52)
1	fresh hot red chili pepper, seeded (see Note)		

Remove and discard the fat from the pork. Slice the pork into ¼-inch matchstick strips. In a medium bowl, mix the salt, pepper, and cornstarch and toss with the pork. Marinate the pork for 20 minutes.

Soak the dried rice noodles in warm tap water for 15 minutes; drain. Rinse well with cold water and drain well. Set aside.

Cut the chili pepper into thin matchstick strips. Cut the green onions into 1½-inch matchstick strips.

Heat a 3-quart saucepan over medium heat and add the vegetable oil. Add the chili paste, garlic, and chili pepper and sauté for 1 minute. Add the chicken broth and bring to a boil.

Add the pork and rice noodles; stir to separate the pork pieces. Return to boiling again and turn off the heat. Add the green onions.

NOTE: Noodles can be thin or wide. If you want the soup spicier, add another pepper.

sun-dried scallops, tofu, and spinach soup

serves 4

If you are not going to serve the soup right away, do not add the spinach until immediately before serving. Just reheat the soup to boiling, add the spinach, and return to a full boil.

4	sun-dried scallops (see Glossary of Ingredients)	1	teaspoon vegetable oil
2	ounces spinach, stemmed	½	teaspoon minced garlic
1	large egg	4	cups Chicken Broth (page 52)
½	teaspoon salt	4	ounces firm tofu, diced
¼	teaspoon white pepper	½	teaspoon sesame oil

Soak the sun-dried scallops in hot water for 20 minutes, or until soft. Remove the muscles from the sides of the scallops; drain. Rinse in warm water; drain.

Rinse the spinach leaves under cold running water to clean.

In a small bowl, beat the egg with salt and pepper.

Heat a 2-quart saucepan over medium heat and add the vegetable oil. When hot, add the garlic and sun-dried scallops and stir-fry for 1 minute. Add the chicken broth and heat to boiling. Turn the heat down to medium-low and simmer for 20 minutes.

Turn the heat up to high and add the tofu and spinach pieces. Return the soup to a boil. Stir the egg mixture slowly into the broth, stirring constantly with a fork until the egg mixture forms threads. Add the sesame oil and remove from the heat. Serve immediately.

tofu tomato soup

serves 4

This soup is full of protein. You may substitute canned tomatoes for fresh to save time.

2	large eggs		4	cups Chicken Broth (page 52)
½	teaspoon salt		10	ounces firm tofu, cut into ¾-inch cubes
3	dried black mushrooms		1	large tomato, cut into ¾-inch cubes
2	teaspoons cornstarch		½	cup fresh or frozen peas

In a small bowl, slightly beat the eggs with the salt. Set aside.

Soak the black mushrooms in hot water for 20 minutes, or until soft. Cut off the stems and discard. Cut the mushroom caps into ½-inch diced pieces.

In a small bowl, mix the cornstarch with 2 teaspoons water.

In a 3-quart soup pot, place the chicken broth and mushrooms. Bring to a boil and cook for 5 minutes. Add the tofu, tomato, and peas and return to a boil. Lower the heat, stir in the cornstarch mixture, and return to high heat. When the soup returns to a rolling boil, pour in a spoonful of the egg mixture, stirring in a circular motion. When shreds have formed, continue to add spoonfuls of the egg mixture to the boiling soup, stirring constantly with a fork until all the egg mixture forms shreds, about 30 seconds. Serve.

tomato beef
egg drop soup

Egg drop soup is a traditional Chinese preparation, and this recipe calls for very common ingredients. Rich in protein, it is a meal in itself.

2	tomatoes	1	teaspoon cornstarch
2	leaves celery cabbage (Napa cabbage)	1	teaspoon vegetable oil
2	eggs	½	teaspoon soy sauce
¼	teaspoon salt, divided	4	cups Beef Broth (page 51) or Chicken Broth
3	ounces beef sirloin or tenderloin		(page 52)
1	teaspoon finely chopped fresh ginger	1	tablespoon chopped green onion, white and
⅛	teaspoon white pepper		green parts

Wash the tomatoes and cut each tomato into 4 wedges. Wash the celery cabbage and cut into thin slices.

In a small bowl, place the eggs and beat with ⅛ teaspoon salt.

Cut the beef into thin slices. In a bowl, mix the ginger, the remaining ⅛ teaspoon salt, the pepper, cornstarch, oil, and soy sauce. Add the beef, toss, and marinate for ½ hour or longer in the refrigerator.

In a 3-quart saucepan, place the beef or chicken broth and bring to a boil. Add the tomatoes and celery cabbage and boil for 1 minute.

Add the marinated beef and bring back to a boil. Stir the egg mixture slowly into the broth, stirring constantly with a fork, until the egg forms threads.

Before serving, garnish with the chopped green onion.

velvet beef
cilantro soup

Cilantro is also known as Chinese parsley. Egg whites create a velvety texture in Chinese cooking.

4	ounces boneless beef sirloin or flank steak	1	small bunch cilantro
1	teaspoon vegetable oil	4	cups Beef Broth (page 51) or Chicken Broth
½	teaspoon salt		(page 52)
2	tablespoons + ½ teaspoon cornstarch, divided	1	teaspoon finely chopped fresh ginger
	Pinch white pepper	2	egg whites, slightly beaten

Cut the beef into very thin slices. In a bowl, mix the vegetable oil, salt, ½ teaspoon cornstarch, and pepper together. Add the beef and toss.

Wash the cilantro several times to remove sand. Break off all but about 1 inch of stems. Break the leaves and remaining stems into small pieces.

Combine 2 tablespoons cornstarch with 2 tablespoons water.

Heat the broth to boiling. Add the beef and return to a boil. Stir in the cornstarch mixture and ginger and bring to a rolling boil. Pour the egg whites slowly into the broth, stirring constantly with a fork until the egg forms threads. Add the cilantro and return to a boil. Turn off the heat and serve.

velvet chicken corn soup

Corn makes a nice addition to this soup. You can use frozen corn if necessary. This soup can be reheated very successfully.

4	ounces skinless, boneless chicken breast	1	teaspoon finely chopped fresh ginger
2	egg whites	2	tablespoons cornstarch
½	teaspoon sesame oil	4	cups Chicken Broth (page 52)
¼	teaspoon salt	¾	cup corn kernels
⅛	teaspoon white pepper	1	tablespoon chopped green onion or cilantro

In a food processor, chop the chicken to a paste. If a food processor isn't available, cut the chicken into very tiny pieces with a sharp knife and place in a bowl. Add the egg whites, sesame oil, salt, pepper, ginger, and cornstarch and mix well to combine all the ingredients.

In a 3-quart saucepan, place the chicken broth and heat to a rolling boil. Slowly add the chicken mixture and the corn to the broth, stirring constantly, and bring to a rolling boil. Turn off the heat. Garnish with green onion or cilantro.

poultry

Barbecued Chicken

Braised Duck with Fermented Red Bean Curd

Chicken with Salted Black Beans, Tomatoes, and
Green Peppers

Chicken with Coconut Sauce

Chicken with Three Mushrooms

Chicken with Shiitake Mushrooms and Snow Peas

Clay Pot Chicken

Curry Chicken in Clay Pot

Diced Chicken with Chili Pepper

Diced Chicken with Vegetables

Drunken Cornish Hens

Fragrant Chicken with Tomatoes

Ginger Pineapple Chicken

Stuffed Cornish Hens

Glazed Cornish Hens

Lychee Duck

Roasted Duck with Beer

Salt and Pepper Quail

Steamed Whole Chicken

Stir-Fried Chicken with Bok Choy

Stir-Fried Chicken with Mango

Stir-Fried Chicken with Pineapple

Stir-Fried Chicken with Red Curry Sauce

Stir-Fried Chicken with Zucchini and Black Bean Sauce

barbecued chicken

You can double the marinade ingredients and use a whole chicken, cut into pieces. Make sure the chicken is completely dry and don't cover it while it's marinating so the skin becomes crispier when it bakes. Cut up leftovers for a simple and healthy Chinese chicken salad the next day.

1   pound whole chicken breast, skin on, bone in

marinade

1	teaspoon salt
2	teaspoons sugar
2	tablespoons ketchup
2	tablespoons hoisin sauce

2	teaspoons minced garlic
1	teaspoon minced fresh ginger
2	teaspoons oyster sauce, plus more for serving if desired

Rinse the chicken with cold water and pat dry with paper towels.

In a small bowl, combine the salt, sugar, ketchup, hoisin sauce, garlic, and ginger and mix well. Rub the marinade over the entire breast and marinate for 30 minutes or longer, refrigerated.

Heat the oven to 400°F. Place the chicken, skin-side up, on a baking pan and bake, uncovered, for 30 minutes. Reduce the oven temperature to 350°F. and bake 15 minutes, or until done. (The meat should reach a temperature of 160 to 170°F.)

Remove the chicken meat from the bone (and remove and discard the skin, if desired). Drizzle with 2 teaspoons oyster sauce. Serve with the oyster sauce or use for salads.

braised duck with fermented red bean curd

Red bean curd can be found at Asian markets in a jar or can. This dish is very rich and is an impressive centerpiece at a dinner party.

2	(6- to 8-ounce) whole boneless duck breasts	4	teaspoons vegetable oil
2	(1-ounce) squares fermented red bean curd	1	tablespoon bourbon
1	tablespoon minced garlic	2	teaspoons soy sauce
2	teaspoons sugar		

Rinse the duck breasts with cold water and pat dry with paper towels. In a small bowl, mash the bean curd; mix in the garlic and sugar.

Heat a nonstick skillet over high heat and add 4 teaspoons vegetable oil. Add the duck breasts and brown both sides (about 2 minutes per side).

Add the bean curd mixture to the duck, cook for 30 seconds, turn over the duck breast, and cook another 10 seconds. Add 1 cup water, cover, and simmer for 20 minutes, skin-side up. Turn the duck over and add the bourbon and soy sauce. Turn the heat up to high and continue to cook an additional 15 minutes, uncovered, reducing the liquid to ½ cup.

Remove from the heat. Cut each breast in half lengthwise and slice the halved duck breasts into ½-inch slices. Arrange the slices on a platter and drizzle the remaining sauce from the pan over them.

chicken with salted black beans, tomatoes, and green peppers

Black beans, which are actually made from soybeans, can be found at Asian markets. You may use black bean sauce found in a jar, which is available in the ethnic section of most grocery stores, as a substitute.

10	ounces skinless, boneless chicken breast	½	cup Chicken Broth (page 52)
¼	teaspoon salt	2	teaspoons soy sauce
	Pinch white pepper	1	tablespoon vegetable oil
2	tablespoons + 1 teaspoon cornstarch, divided	1	small white onion, cubed
3	small tomatoes	1	teaspoon minced garlic
2	tablespoons salted black beans	1	teaspoon finely chopped fresh ginger
1	tablespoon sugar	1	green bell pepper, cored, seeded, and cubed

Cut the chicken into ¾-inch cubes. In a medium bowl, combine the salt, pepper, and 1 teaspoon cornstarch. Stir in the chicken, cover, and refrigerate for 30 minutes.

Cut each tomato into 6 wedges.

In a small bowl, place the beans and cover with warm water. Soak the beans for 10 minutes. Remove the beans from the water and rinse with cold water to remove any excess salt and loosen the skins. Drain well.

In a small bowl, mix together the remaining 2 tablespoons cornstarch, sugar, chicken broth, and soy sauce. Set aside.

Heat a large nonstick skillet over high heat. Add the vegetable oil. Add the chicken, onion, black beans, garlic, and ginger; cook for 2 minutes, or until the chicken turns white. Push the chicken to the sides of the skillet and add the tomatoes and green pepper to the center of the skillet. Stir and cook 2 minutes. Add the cornstarch mixture and stir the chicken, tomatoes, and green pepper together, mixing well. When the sauce is thickened, about 2 minutes, turn off the heat. Place on a serving platter.

chicken with
coconut sauce

serves 4

This is a convenient dish to prepare ahead. Since the chicken must be fried twice, you can prefry the chicken pieces and store them up to 5 months in the freezer. Thaw pieces in the refrigerator overnight and at dinnertime, you simply refry the chicken in hot oil, prepare the coconut sauce, and you've got a fast, delicious dinner. For proper deep-frying technique, see photo insert.

1	pound skinless, boneless chicken breast
1	small egg
4	tablespoons cornstarch, divided
1¼	teaspoons salt, divided
¼	teaspoon white pepper
1	teaspoon finely chopped fresh ginger
3	to 4 cups vegetable oil, divided
¼	cup all-purpose flour
¼	teaspoon baking soda

coconut sauce

1	tablespoon oil
1	teaspoon minced garlic
¾	cup Chicken Broth (page 52)
¾	cup coconut milk
¼	cup fresh lime juice
¼	cup sugar
2	tablespoons vinegar

garnish

6	maraschino cherries (optional)
1	lime, thinly sliced

Cut the chicken in half lengthwise and pound to flatten the thick part so the chicken is of consistent thickness. Place the chicken in a shallow dish. In a small bowl, mix together the egg, 2 teaspoons cornstarch, 1 teaspoon salt, the pepper, and the ginger. Pour the egg mixture over the chicken, turning the chicken to coat all sides. Cover and refrigerate 30 minutes. Remove the chicken from the marinade; reserve the marinade. In a small bowl, mix together 4 teaspoons cornstarch and 4 teaspoons water. Set aside.

To prepare the sauce, in a small saucepan over high heat, add 1 tablespoon oil and the garlic. Cook the garlic until fragrant, 10 to 15 seconds (do not brown). Add the chicken broth, coconut milk, lime juice, sugar, and vinegar and bring to a boil. Stir in the cornstarch mixture. Cook and stir until thickened, about 10 seconds.

Heat all but 2 tablespoons of the vegetable oil, 1 to 1½ inches deep, in a wok to 350°F. (If using a skillet, be sure to use a pan 4 inches deep to prevent splattering.) Mix the reserved marinade, the flour, ¼ cup water, the remaining 2 tablespoons cornstarch, 2 tablespoons vegetable oil, the baking soda, and the remaining ¼ teaspoon salt. One at a time, dip the chicken pieces into the batter to coat all sides. Fry the chicken pieces for about 3 minutes, or until light brown, turning 2 to 3 times. Drain on paper towels.

Increase the oil temperature to 375°F. Fry the chicken pieces again until golden brown, turning once, about 2 minutes. Drain on paper towels. Using a very sharp knife, cut each piece crosswise into ¾-inch pieces. Place in a single layer on a heated platter. Reheat the sauce over high heat and pour over the chicken.

Garnish the edge of the platter with the cherries, if using, and thin slices of lime.

chicken with three mushrooms

serves 2

You may use any variety of mushrooms for this dish. There is such a diverse selection at most supermarkets these days, you can have fun and be creative.

8	ounces skinless, boneless chicken breast		1	ounce shiitake mushrooms
¼	teaspoon salt		1	ounce oyster mushrooms
	Dash white pepper		1	ounce white mushrooms
2	tablespoons + 1 teaspoon cornstarch, divided		4	teaspoons vegetable oil
4	ounces snow peas		1	teaspoon chopped fresh ginger
1	cup Chicken Broth (page 52)		2	garlic cloves, minced
2	tablespoons oyster sauce		¼	cup shredded green onions, white part only
½	teaspoon sugar			

Cut the chicken into 2 × ¼-inch-thin slices. In a glass or plastic bowl, mix the salt, pepper, and 1 teaspoon cornstarch. Stir in the chicken and set aside.

Remove the strings from the snow peas. Bring a small pot of water to a boil, place the snow peas in the boiling water, and return to boiling. Remove from the heat; drain. Immediately rinse with cold water until the peas are cold; drain. In a small bowl, mix the chicken broth, the remaining 2 tablespoons cornstarch, the oyster sauce, and sugar. Quickly rinse all the mushrooms with cold water and pat dry. Cut off and discard the stems. Cut the caps into ¾-inch strips.

Heat a wok or nonstick pan over high heat. Add the vegetable oil and the chicken. Cook and stir until the chicken turns white, about 1 minute. Add the ginger, garlic, and mushrooms; stir and cook for 1 minute. Add the chicken broth mixture and cook and stir until thickened. Add the snow peas and stir for 30 seconds. Remove to a heated platter and garnish with the shredded green onions.

chicken with shiitake mushrooms and snow peas

serves 2

This recipe is very healthy and easy to prepare. In a Chinese home, it is often accompanied by steamed or panfried fish and will serve 4 to 6, with white rice. If the preparation is done ahead, actual cooking time is about 10 minutes.

8	ounces skinless, boneless chicken breast	½	teaspoon sugar
¼	teaspoon salt	4	teaspoons vegetable oil
	Dash white pepper	1	teaspoon finely chopped fresh ginger
3	teaspoons cornstarch, divided	1	teaspoon minced garlic
4	ounces shiitake mushrooms	½	cup Chicken Broth (page 52)
4	ounces snow peas	1	(2-inch) piece green onion, shredded
1	tablespoon oyster sauce		

Cut the chicken into 2 × ¼-inch slices. In a bowl, mix the salt, pepper, and 1 teaspoon cornstarch. Stir in the chicken.

Cut off and discard the stems from the mushrooms. Rinse the mushroom caps in cold water, pat dry, and cut into ½-inch strips.

Remove the strings from the snow peas. Bring a small pot of water to a boil, place the snow peas in the boiling water, and return to boiling. Immediately remove from the heat; drain. Immediately rinse with cold water; drain. In a small bowl, mix 2 teaspoons water, the remaining 2 teaspoons cornstarch, the oyster sauce, and sugar.

Heat a wok or nonstick pan over high heat. Add the vegetable oil and chicken and cook and stir until the chicken turns white, about 2 minutes. Add the ginger, garlic, and mushrooms and stir and cook for 1 minute. Add the chicken broth, cover, and cook for 1 minute. Stir in the cornstarch mixture; cook and stir until thickened. Add the snow peas; stir and cook for 30 seconds. Remove to a heated platter and garnish with the shredded green onion.

clay pot chicken

Clay pots are popular in China as they retain heat and can go straight from the oven to the din-
ner table. Meat is usually seared and then simmered slowly in the pot in the oven to create a ten-
der and flavorful dish. While the clay pot dish simmers in the oven, you may prepare a stir-fry
dish that will be ready at the same time.

1	pound skinless, boneless chicken thighs	½	teaspoon sugar
½	teaspoon salt	1	tablespoon vegetable oil
⅛	teaspoon white pepper	1	teaspoon minced garlic
1	tablespoon cornstarch	1	teaspoon finely chopped fresh ginger
4	large dried black mushrooms	1	small carrot, peeled and thinly sliced
10	ounces firm tofu	2	to 3 green onions, with tops, cut into
2	tablespoons oyster sauce		1-inch pieces
2	teaspoons soy sauce		

Preheat the oven to 400°F. Place a 2-quart clay pot or a heavy casserole pot with a cover in the oven to heat.

Trim the fat from the chicken and cut the chicken into 1-inch cubes. In a bowl, combine the salt, pepper, and cornstarch. Toss the chicken with the cornstarch mixture and set aside.

Soak the black mushrooms in hot water for 20 minutes, or until soft. Drain and rinse with cold water. Remove and discard the stems. Cut the caps into ½-inch pieces. Cut the tofu into ¾-inch cubes. In a small bowl, mix the oyster sauce, soy sauce, and sugar. Set aside.

Heat a nonstick skillet or wok over high heat and add the vegetable oil, garlic, ginger, and chicken. Stir-fry for 1 minute. Add the black mushrooms, tofu, and carrot, and continue to stir 1 more minute. Stir in the oyster sauce mixture and green onions and mix well. Turn off the heat and transfer everything into the preheated clay pot. Cover and place in the preheated oven for 15 to 20 minutes. Serve hot.

To hold the finished dish, turn the oven off and keep warm until ready to serve.

curry chicken in clay pot

White onions and tomatoes bring out the flavor of curry. Curry originated in India, but it has been used in China for centuries. This is a hearty and comforting dish, especially in the wintertime. You may also use canned tomatoes in this recipe. Increase or decrease the amount of curry according to taste.

1	pound skinless, boneless chicken thighs	2	teaspoons minced garlic
¼	teaspoon salt	1	medium onion, thinly sliced
⅛	teaspoon white pepper	2	tablespoons curry powder
1	teaspoon finely chopped fresh ginger	1	medium tomato, cut into ½-inch wedges
1	tablespoon cornstarch	1	tablespoon soy sauce
6	small new red potatoes, cut into ½-inch slices	1	teaspoon sugar
1	small carrot, peeled and cut into ¼-inch slices	1	green onion, with top, cut into 1-inch pieces
2	tablespoons vegetable oil		

Preheat the oven to 400°F. Place a 2-quart clay pot or heavy casserole with a cover in the oven to heat.

Trim the fat from the chicken and cut the chicken into 1-inch cubes. In a bowl, combine the salt, pepper, ginger, and cornstarch. Toss the chicken with the cornstarch mixture and set aside.

Bring 2 cups water to a boil in a saucepan over high heat. Add the potatoes and carrot, cover, and cook 2 minutes. Drain and set aside.

Heat a nonstick skillet or wok over high heat until hot. Add the vegetable oil and the chicken; stir and cook until lightly browned, about 1 minute. Add the garlic, onion, curry powder, and tomato and stir-fry 1 minute. Add the potatoes, carrot, soy sauce, and sugar and continue to stir until well mixed. Turn off the heat and transfer the mixture to the preheated clay pot. Cover the clay pot and return to the preheated oven for 15 to 20 minutes. Serve hot.

To hold the finished dish, turn the oven off and keep warm until ready to serve. Stir in the green onion just before serving.

diced chicken with chili pepper

This is a very fast dish to prepare. Nuts like cashews or peanuts are an excellent addition to this recipe. Add more chili peppers if you want a spicier dish. Serve Chinese or Thai beer as the perfect complement to the fiery flavors.

1	pound skinless, boneless chicken breast	2	small hot red chili peppers, chopped
¼	teaspoon salt	1	teaspoon minced garlic
	Dash white pepper	1	teaspoon finely chopped fresh ginger
2	teaspoons cornstarch	2	tablespoons hoisin sauce
2	tablespoons vegetable oil	1	tablespoon soy sauce
¼	cup diced onion	2	tablespoons chopped green onion

Cut the chicken into ½-inch cubes. In a medium bowl, mix the salt, pepper, and cornstarch together. Toss the mixture with the chicken and set aside.

Heat a wok or nonstick skillet over high heat and add the vegetable oil. Add the chicken, onion, chili peppers, garlic, and ginger and cook until the chicken turns white, stirring to separate the pieces, about 2 minutes. Add the hoisin sauce and soy sauce and continue to cook for 2 minutes. Remove from the heat and place on a serving platter. Garnish with the green onion.

diced chicken with vegetables

By dicing all the ingredients in a stir-fry to approximately the same size (see photo insert), every-thing is cooked evenly and quickly. You may use fresh or frozen peas for this dish, and feel free to substitute or add other types of vegetables. This is a popular everyday dish that kids love, and a great way to get them to eat their vegetables. Serve over hot, steaming rice for a quick lunchtime rice bowl.

8	ounces skinless, boneless chicken breast	½	teaspoon sugar
½	teaspoon salt	2	tablespoons vegetable oil
	Dash white pepper	¼	cup diced onion
2	tablespoons + 1 teaspoon cornstarch, divided	1	teaspoon minced garlic
½	cup diced carrots	1	teaspoon finely chopped fresh ginger
1	cup diced celery (use the tender heart center)	1	(4-ounce) can button mushrooms, drained
2	tablespoons oyster sauce	¼	cup chopped green onions
1¼	cups Chicken Broth (page 52), divided		

Cut the chicken into ½-inch pieces. In a medium bowl, combine the salt, pepper, and 1 teaspoon cornstarch. Stir in the chicken, cover, and refrigerate for 20 minutes.

Bring a small saucepan of water to a boil. Add the carrots and celery and return to a boil. Cover and cook for 1 minute. Immediately drain and rinse in cold water; drain. In a small bowl, mix the oyster sauce, the remaining 2 tablespoons cornstarch, ¼ cup chicken broth, and the sugar. Set aside.

Heat a wok or nonstick pan over high heat until very hot. Add 1 tablespoon vegetable oil and the chicken pieces and cook until the chicken turns white, stirring to separate the pieces, about 2 minutes. Remove the chicken from the pan.

Reheat the wok or pan over high heat. Add the remaining 1 tablespoon vegetable oil, the onion, garlic, and ginger; cook for 1 minute. Add the celery, carrots, and mushrooms and cook for 1 minute. Add the chicken and the remaining 1 cup chicken broth. Cook until the broth comes to a boil. Stir in the cornstarch mixture and cook and stir until thickened, about 2 minutes. Remove from the heat. Garnish with the green onions.

drunken cornish hens

Keep Cornish game hens on hand in your freezer to make this impressive dish with just a handful of pantry ingredients. They can be served whole or cut into pieces; Chinese people normally cut Cornish hens through the bone into 2-inch pieces. You may make Sober Cornish Hens without the wine for children. This dish can be served hot or cold. If you have two steamers, you can cook all four hens at once.

4	(1½- to 2-pound) Cornish game hens	¼	teaspoon white pepper
4	teaspoons salt	4	green onions, halved
¼	teaspoon five-spice powder	1	teaspoon vegetable oil
4	teaspoons finely chopped fresh ginger	2	cups dry white wine or Shaoxing rice wine

Wash each hen, cleaning the cavity very well. Dry completely with paper towels.

In a small bowl, combine the salt, five-spice powder, ginger, and pepper. Place ¼ of the seasonings in your hand and rub the inside and outside of the hen. Repeat the procedure for each hen.

Place 1 green onion in the cavity of each hen, place the hens in the refrigerator, and refrigerate for at least 1 hour and up to 1 day.

Brush vegetable oil over each hen, then place 2 hens on a heatproof platter and put in a large steamer rack; steam over boiling water for 30 minutes (steam longer if the Cornish hens are larger than average). Remove the hens from the steamer, pour the wine over the hens, and let sit in the wine for 30 minutes. Baste every 10 minutes. Remove the onion from the cavity. Meanwhile, cook the other 2 hens.

Cut each hen in half through the breast. Turn it over and cut through the backbone. Cut off the wing, leg, and thigh. Cut the breast away from the back. Cut the back into 3 pieces and place in the lower center of the platter.

Cut the breast into 3 or 4 pieces and arrange toward the top of the platter above the back pieces. Arrange the wings on each side near the breast pieces and the legs and thighs at an angle near the backbone pieces. Serve.

fragrant chicken with tomatoes

serves 4

Use firm ripe tomatoes for this quick and healthy dish. This recipe is extremely versatile and flexible as you stir-fry the chicken first, allowing you to use as many vegetables as you like and improvise with the variety. You can use more garlic, ginger, and cilantro to enhance this fragrant dish.

10	ounces skinless, boneless chicken breast	1	tablespoon soy sauce
¼	teaspoon salt	2	tablespoons vegetable oil, divided
⅛	teaspoon white pepper	1	teaspoon finely chopped fresh ginger
2	tablespoons cornstarch, divided	2	teaspoons minced garlic
3	small tomatoes	½	cup Chicken Broth (page 52)
1	small white onion	4	to 5 green onions, with tops, cut into 1-inch
1	teaspoon sugar		pieces (about 1 cup)

Cut the chicken into ¾-inch pieces. In a medium bowl, combine the salt, pepper, and 2 teaspoons cornstarch. Add the chicken pieces and cover and refrigerate for 30 minutes. Cut each tomato into 8 wedges. Cut the white onion into 1-inch squares. Mix together the remaining 4 teaspoons cornstarch, the sugar, 1 tablespoon water, and the soy sauce; set aside.

Heat a wok or nonstick pan over high heat until hot. Add 1 tablespoon vegetable oil and the chicken; stir-fry for 2 minutes, or until the chicken turns white. Remove the chicken from the pan.

Reheat the pan over high heat. Add the remaining 1 tablespoon vegetable oil, the white onions, ginger, and garlic and stir for 20 seconds. Add the tomatoes and continue stirring for 30 seconds. Add the cooked chicken and broth and heat to boiling. Stir in the cornstarch mixture; cook and stir for 30 seconds, or until thickened. Add the green onions and cook for an additional 15 seconds. Serve hot.

84

everyday chinese cooking

ginger pineapple chicken

Try fresh orange sections and orange juice instead of the pineapple chunks and lemon juice. This chicken goes very well with a simple stir-fry vegetable dish or over sautéed mixed greens. We recommend using a nonstick skillet for this dish. When using chopsticks, it's ideal to slice the chicken after it is cooked, or you may serve the breasts whole when using forks and knives.

1	pound skinless, boneless chicken breast	1	teaspoon minced garlic
2	teaspoons finely chopped fresh ginger, divided	1	tablespoon + 2 teaspoons lemon juice, divided
1	small egg white	1	tablespoon ketchup
½	teaspoon salt	2	teaspoons sugar
	Dash white pepper	1¼	cups Chicken Broth (page 52), divided
2	tablespoons cornstarch, divided	1	cup canned or fresh pineapple chunks
¼	cup all-purpose flour	2	tablespoons minced fresh chives
2	tablespoons vegetable oil, divided		

Dry the chicken and pound the thicker side of the breast so that the chicken will cook evenly. In a medium bowl, mix together 1 teaspoon ginger, the egg white, salt, pepper, and 2 teaspoons cornstarch. Add the chicken and turn to coat well. Set aside.

In a small bowl, mix the remaining 4 teaspoons cornstarch with 4 teaspoons water. Set aside.

Place the flour on a piece of wax paper, add the chicken to the flour, and turn to coat both sides of the chicken.

Heat a small saucepan over high heat. Add 1 teaspoon vegetable oil, the garlic, the remaining 1 teaspoon ginger, 1 tablespoon lemon juice, the ketchup, sugar, and 1 cup chicken broth and bring to a boil. Stir in the cornstarch mixture; continue to stir and cook until the sauce thickens. Add the pineapple chunks to the sauce. Bring the sauce back to a boil and turn off the heat. Set aside.

Heat a large nonstick skillet over medium heat; add 1 tablespoon vegetable oil and the chicken pieces. Panfry 1 minute per side. Add the remaining 2 teaspoons vegetable oil, 2 teaspoons lemon juice, and ¼ cup chicken broth and cook until the liquid is absorbed, about 3 minutes. Remove the chicken from the skillet and cut each piece crosswise into ¾-inch pieces. Reheat the sauce to boiling and pour over the chicken. Garnish with the chives.

stuffed cornish hens

Save time by preparing the stuffing and gravy the night before for this fun and interesting dish. When you're ready to serve, steam the Cornish game hens and reheat the sauce. Serve with a light vegetable stir-fry to complete your dinner party menu.

6	medium dried black mushrooms	½	cup diced bamboo shoots
2	(1½- to 2-pound) Cornish game hens	5	tablespoons cornstarch, divided
2	teaspoons vegetable oil	1½	teaspoons salt
2	teaspoons light soy sauce	½	teaspoon white pepper, divided
2	green onions	6	ounces soft tofu, mashed
1	large egg white	1½	cups Chicken Broth (page 52)
1	teaspoon finely chopped fresh ginger	2	tablespoons oyster sauce

Soak the mushrooms in hot water for 15 to 20 minutes, or until soft. Rinse in cold water and drain. Squeeze out any excess water. Remove and discard the stems and cut the caps into ¼-inch pieces.

Run the hens under cold water and dry with paper towels. With the hen breast-side down, cut through the backbones. Turn over and place, bone-side down, on the cutting board. Using a very sharp knife, lift the skin up and detach the skin from the bones, working the skin off the meat to the thigh joint. Slice off the leg at the thigh joint (not through the skin) and repeat with the wing joint, so that the legs and wings remain in the skin. Remove the skin totally from the carcass. You will end up with the legs and wings still in the skin as one whole piece. Remove the breast and thigh meat from the bones and cut into ¼-inch diced pieces.

Mix the 2 skins of the game hens with the oil and light soy sauce.

To prepare the stuffing, dice the white part of the green onions. Thinly slice the green tops lengthwise into strips 2 inches long. Place the green tops in a bowl of ice water and reserve to use as a garnish.

Mix the diced meat with the egg white, diced onions, ginger, bamboo shoots, mushrooms, 3 tablespoons cornstarch, salt, ¼ teaspoon pepper, and the mashed tofu. Mix very well and divide in half. Place the stuffing in the breast and thigh skin of the game hens, shaping to the form of the original hen. Place the game hens on a heatproof platter and steam over boiling water for 30 minutes on high heat.

Meanwhile, in a small saucepan, combine the chicken broth, oyster sauce, and the remaining ¼ teaspoon pepper and bring to a boil. In a small bowl, mix together the remaining 2 tablespoons cornstarch and 2 tablespoons water and stir into the chicken broth. Cook until the sauce thickens, about 1 minute, and remove from the heat. Serve the sauce over or alongside the hens. Garnish with the reserved green onions.

glazed cornish hens

serves 4

You can store the soy sauce mixture in an airtight container in the refrigerator for up to 4 weeks and use it again. Use leftovers for a quick salad or flavorful sandwich.

4	(1½- to 2-pound) Cornish game hens	¾	cup sugar
1½	cups soy sauce	4	star anise
½	cup dry white wine	8	to 10 (1 × ⅛-inch) pieces fresh ginger

Remove the excess fat from the Cornish hens. Wash the hens in cold running water; drain.

In a 3-quart saucepan, heat the soy sauce, 2 cups water, the wine, sugar, star anise, and ginger to boiling. The saucepan should be large enough to hold 2 hens, side by side, on the bottom.

Add 2 hens and return the sauce to boiling. Turn the hens over, being careful not to break the skin. Return to boiling and reduce the heat to medium and simmer 5 minutes. Reduce the heat to low, cover, and simmer 15 to 20 minutes, or until done. Do not allow the mixture to boil too hard or the skin on the hens will break. Remove the hens carefully to prevent the skin from breaking; keep warm.

Repeat with the remaining hens. Cut each hen into halves and serve warm.

lychee duck

Canned mandarin oranges or pineapple chunks can be used instead of the lychees.

1	(½-pound) boneless roasted duck breast (page 89)	1	tablespoon white vinegar
		1	tablespoon vegetable oil
		1	teaspoon soy sauce
sauce		1	teaspoon minced garlic
2	tablespoons cornstarch	1	(14-ounce) can lychees, drained
⅓	cup Chicken Broth (page 52)		
⅓	cup sugar	10	maraschino cherries
⅓	cup lemon juice		

Cut the roasted duck breast in half, then cut into ½-inch slices. Arrange on a serving platter.

In a small bowl, mix together the cornstarch and 2 tablespoons water and set aside.

In a small saucepan, combine the chicken broth, sugar, lemon juice, vinegar, vegetable oil, soy sauce, and garlic and bring to a boil. Add the cornstarch mixture, stirring constantly until thickened. Add the lychees and return to a boil again. Pour over the duck breast slices and garnish with the cherries.

roasted duck with beer

This dish can be served hot, or slice the cold duck thinly over a salad or over stir-fried vegetables. For company or a weeknight dinner you can prepare the duck breasts ahead and simply reheat them in the oven. Serve either hot or cold with apricot or plum sauce. This goes great with Tsing Tao beer or a dark German ale.

3   (½-pound) boneless whole duck breasts

marinade

½   cup soy sauce (don't use light soy sauce)
1   cup beer (Tsing Tao or German ale)
4   to 5 whole star anise cloves or 1 teaspoon broken pieces

1   tablespoon sugar
1   tablespoon chopped fresh ginger
1   tablespoon minced garlic

Rinse the duck breasts with cold water and pat dry with paper towels. In a 9 × 13-inch cake pan, combine the soy sauce, beer, star anise, sugar, ginger, and garlic together thoroughly. Marinate the duck in the soy sauce mixture in the refrigerator for 4 hours, turning over 2 or 3 times. Drain off all of the marinade and discard. Pat the duck dry with paper towels. Refrigerate, uncovered, for 2 hours or overnight. The skin must be completely dry.

Preheat the oven to 425°F. With the skin-side up, cook the duck for 30 minutes. Reduce the heat to 350°F. and cook for an additional 20 minutes, or until the duck skin is golden brown and crispy. Cut each breast in half lengthwise, then cut into ½-inch slices.

salt and pepper quail

Quail can be found in the frozen section of most grocery stores and fresh at some butchers. This dish is quite simple and can be served as an appetizer for four. It's a tasty and impressive dish— great for entertaining and actually very economical too. You may marinate the quail the night before.

4   quail (1 to 1½ pounds total)

marinade

1	teaspoon salt	3	cups + 1 tablespoon vegetable oil, divided
½	teaspoon sugar	1	teaspoon minced garlic
½	teaspoon white pepper	¼	cup minced green onions
¼	teaspoon five-spice powder	2	small diced Thai hot red chili peppers (¼ cup)

Cut each quail in half, rinse with cold water, and pat dry with paper towels.

In a small bowl, combine the salt, sugar, pepper, and five-spice powder and coat the entire quail with this mixture. Marinate for 1 hour or longer, skin-side up, on a tray in the refrigerator. Make sure the skin is dry.

In a wok or large nonstick skillet, heat 3 cups vegetable oil to 375°F. and deep-fry the quail in batches for 3 to 4 minutes, or until golden brown, turning continuously. Remove the quail and drain on paper towels. Remove the oil and reheat the wok over medium heat. Add the remaining 1 tablespoon oil, the garlic, green onions, and chili peppers. Stir and cook until fragrant, about 1 minute. Add the quail to the wok and toss about 30 seconds. Remove and serve hot.

steamed whole chicken

Steaming is one of the healthiest methods of preparation in Chinese cooking. This dish is served often in Chinese homes on special occasions and is usually accompanied by stir-fried vegetables and rice to make the meal complete.

1   whole chicken breast (about 1 pound)

marinade
½   teaspoon salt
1   teaspoon white wine
1   teaspoon light soy sauce
½   teaspoon sugar
⅛   teaspoon white pepper
1   teaspoon finely chopped fresh ginger

1   tablespoon oyster sauce
2   tablespoons chopped green onion, with tops

Rinse the chicken with cold water and pat dry with paper towels.

In a medium bowl, mix together the salt, white wine, soy sauce, sugar, pepper, and ginger. Add the chicken, turn to coat, and marinate for 30 minutes in the refrigerator.

Place the chicken in a 9-inch pie plate. Put the plate on a rack in a steamer, cover, and steam over boiling water for 20 minutes. Remove any juice to a small bowl and mix with the oyster sauce. Set aside.

Remove the skin and bones from the cooked chicken breast. Cut into 2 × ½-inch pieces. Place the chicken slices on a platter and pour the sauce over. Garnish with the chopped green onion.

stir-fried chicken with bok choy

serves 4

Bok choy can be found in most grocery stores. You may use baby bok choy if you prefer, but cut it into 1-inch pieces instead of thin slices. For family cooking, we recommend using both the white and green sections. Use any remaining bok choy the next day or add to chicken broth for a flavorful soup.

10	ounces skinless, boneless chicken breast		2	tablespoons oyster sauce
½	teaspoon salt, divided		½	teaspoon sugar
	Dash white pepper		3	tablespoons vegetable oil, divided
4	teaspoons cornstarch, divided		1	teaspoon finely chopped fresh ginger
10	ounces bok choy (4 to 5 stalks)		1	teaspoon minced garlic
4	ounces snow peas		½	cup Chicken Broth (page 52)
1	small red bell pepper			

Cut the chicken into 2 × ½-inch slices. Sprinkle ¼ teaspoon salt, the white pepper, and 1 teaspoon cornstarch over the chicken pieces and set aside.

Wash the bok choy very well and dry with paper towels. Trim off most of the leaves (save for soup or other use). Cut the bok choy stalks diagonally into ½-inch slices.

Remove the strings from the snow peas. Bring a small saucepan of water to a boil. Add the snow peas, cover, and cook for 1 minute. Immediately drain and rinse in cold water; drain.

Core and seed the red bell pepper and cut into 2 × ½-inch strips.

In a small bowl, mix together the oyster sauce, sugar, the remaining 1 tablespoon cornstarch, and 1 tablespoon water.

Heat a wok or nonstick skillet over high heat. Add 2 tablespoons vegetable oil, the ginger, garlic, and chicken. Stir-fry the chicken until it turns white, about 2 minutes. Remove the chicken from the wok and place in a bowl. Reheat the wok and add the remaining 1 tablespoon vegetable oil. Add the bok choy and stir-fry for 1 minute. Add the remaining ¼ teaspoon salt, the chicken broth, and the cooked chicken; stir and cook until the sauce comes to a boil. Stir in the cornstarch mixture and cook 1 minute to thicken. Add the red pepper and snow peas; continue cooking for 1 more minute. Serve.

stir-fried chicken with mango

This colorful recipe is a nice complement to a stir-fried beef or shrimp with vegetable dish. You may use canned mango if fresh mangos are unavailable.

1	pound skinless, boneless chicken breast	2	teaspoons hot red pepper sauce
½	teaspoon salt	2	teaspoons sugar
¼	teaspoon white pepper	1	teaspoon soy sauce
1	teaspoon finely chopped fresh ginger	1	mango
1	small egg white	1	small green bell pepper
2	tablespoons white wine	2	tablespoons all-purpose flour
1	teaspoon minced garlic	2	tablespoons cornstarch
4	tablespoons ketchup	2	teaspoons vegetable oil

Trim the fat from the chicken and cut the chicken into 2 × ½-inch strips. In a medium bowl, mix together the salt, white pepper, ginger, and egg white. Add the chicken, toss, cover, and refrigerate for 20 minutes.

In a small bowl, combine the white wine, garlic, ketchup, red pepper sauce, sugar, and soy sauce. Set aside.

Peel the mango and cut into 2 × ½-inch strips. Place the mango strips in a bowl of hot water for 10 minutes; drain. Core and seed the green pepper and cut into 2 × ½-inch strips.

In a small bowl, mix the flour and cornstarch together. Toss with the marinated chicken to coat and set aside.

Heat a nonstick skillet over medium heat. Add the vegetable oil and chicken pieces. Stir and separate the chicken pieces. Cook for 2 minutes. Add the sauce mixture and green pepper and stir well. Cook for 1 minute and add the mango. Cook and stir until well mixed, about 30 seconds. Remove to a heated serving platter.

stir-fried chicken with pineapple

Read this recipe thoroughly and have all the ingredients organized and ready, as the actual stir-frying time for this dish is very fast.

10	ounces skinless, boneless chicken breast	2	tablespoons vinegar
½	teaspoon salt	1	teaspoon soy sauce
⅛	teaspoon white pepper	2	tablespoons vegetable oil
1	teaspoon minced fresh ginger	1	teaspoon minced garlic
4	teaspoons cornstarch, divided	7	ounces pineapple chunks
¼	cup Chicken Broth (page 52)	2	green onions, with tops, cut into 1-inch slices
2	tablespoons sugar		

Cut the chicken into ¾-inch pieces. In a medium bowl, mix together the salt, pepper, ginger, and 1 teaspoon cornstarch. Add the chicken and toss. Set aside.

In a bowl, combine the chicken broth, sugar, vinegar, soy sauce, and the remaining 1 tablespoon cornstarch and set aside.

Heat a wok or nonstick skillet over high heat and add the vegetable oil and garlic. Add the chicken pieces and stir-fry for 1 minute, or until the chicken turns white.

Add the pineapple chunks and green onions; stir-fry for about 2 minutes. Stir in the cornstarch mixture and continue cooking until the sauce thickens, about 2 minutes. Serve.

stir-fried chicken with red curry sauce

When I was a young girl growing up in China, my grandfather had a good friend from India. He would visit us often and told us how important it was to sauté the curry powder with onions, garlic, and tomatoes to bring out the rich flavor of curry dishes. There are several different types of curry powder, so sample some to find the one that suits your taste. This recipe is not spicy, but you can add chili pepper to make it as spicy as you want.

10	ounces skinless, boneless chicken thighs		1	small white onion
¼	teaspoon salt		1	medium tomato
	Pinch white pepper		1	tablespoon + 2 teaspoons vegetable oil, divided
½	teaspoon finely chopped fresh ginger		2	teaspoons minced garlic
2	teaspoons cornstarch		2	tablespoons curry powder
1	potato		1	teaspoon soy sauce
1	small green zucchini			

Trim the fat from the chicken and cut the chicken into 2 × ½-inch slices. In a medium bowl, combine the salt, pepper, ginger, and cornstarch. Stir in the chicken, cover, and refrigerate for 20 minutes.

Peel the potato and cut into 2 × ¼-inch slices. Blanch the potato slices in boiling water for 1 minute over high heat. Drain and set aside.

Wash the zucchini. Cut off and discard the ends of the zucchini and cut the zucchini into 2 × ½-inch slices. Cut the white onion into ¼-inch slices. Cut the tomato into 8 wedges.

Heat a nonstick skillet over high heat. Add 1 tablespoon vegetable oil and the chicken pieces; stir-fry for 1 minute.

Add the potato, zucchini, tomato, onion, garlic, and curry powder and cook for 2 minutes, stirring constantly. If the mixture is cooking too quickly, turn the heat down. Add the remaining 2 teaspoons vegetable oil and the soy sauce and stir until well mixed. Serve.

stir-fried chicken with zucchini and black bean sauce

serves 4

This is a great summertime dish, when zucchini is bountiful. For a heartier dish, substitute beef for the chicken.

8	ounces skinless, boneless chicken thighs	1	small white onion
1½	teaspoons finely chopped fresh ginger, divided	2	tablespoons salted black beans
¼	teaspoon salt	1	tablespoon soy sauce
⅛	teaspoon white pepper	½	teaspoon sugar
4	teaspoons cornstarch, divided	4	teaspoons vegetable oil, divided
½	pound green zucchini	½	teaspoon minced garlic
½	pound yellow squash	½	cup Chicken Broth (page 52)

Trim the fat off the chicken and cut the chicken into ¾-inch pieces. In a medium bowl, mix together ½ teaspoon chopped ginger, the salt, pepper, and 1 teaspoon cornstarch. Add the chicken and toss. Cover and refrigerate for 20 minutes.

Wash the zucchini and squash. Cut off the ends of the zucchini and squash. Cut the zucchini and squash in half lengthwise and cut each half into ¼-inch diagonal slices. Cut the white onion into ¼-inch slices. Place the salted black beans in a small bowl and cover with warm water. Remove any bean skins that float to the top. Remove the beans from the water, rinse 2 to 3 times with cold water, and drain well. In a small bowl, combine the remaining 1 table-spoon cornstarch, 1 tablespoon water, the soy sauce, and sugar.

Heat a wok or nonstick skillet over high heat and add 2 teaspoons vegetable oil. Add the chicken pieces and cook until white, approximately 3 minutes. Remove the chicken from the wok.

Reheat the wok or skillet and add the remaining 2 teaspoons vegetable oil over high heat. Add the onion, garlic, the remaining 1 teaspoon ginger, and the black beans and cook for 1 minute. Add the zucchini and yellow squash, stirring constantly for 2 minutes. Add the chicken broth and bring to a boil. Add the chicken and stir in the cornstarch mixture. Cook and stir for 30 seconds, or until thickened. Serve hot.

tofu tomato soup (*page 68*)

chicken, bok choy, and
clam soup (*page 56*)

clockwise from top left:
spicy beef skewers (*page 42*); lettuce cups with turkey (*page 38*);
firecracker shrimp (*page 40*); and panfried pork dumplings (*page 39*)

chicken with coconut sauce
(*page 76*)

stir-fried chicken
with mango (*page 93*)

curry chicken in clay pot
(*page 80*)

shredded beef with red jalapeño peppers *(page 104)*

stir-fried beef with tomato
and basil *(page 107)*

pork medallions with
peking sauce *(page 113)*

sizzling garlic pork (*page 116*)

braided fish steamed with
ginger and green onions (*page 124*)

tea-smoked sea bass (*page 143*)

beef

Barbecued Beef

Basil Beef

Beef Tenderloin with Leek

Beef with Hot Peppers

Braised Beef Shank

Braised Chuck Roast with Daikon Radish

Shredded Beef with Red Jalapeño Peppers

Steak, Mongolian Style

Stir-Fried Beef with Brussels Sprouts

Stir-Fried Beef with Tomato and Basil

barbecued beef

serves 4 to 6

This beef can be marinated in the refrigerator up to 24 hours in advance. Prepare a light and healthy side dish by stir-frying seasonal vegetables while the beef is grilling. Tsing Tao beer is a wonderful complement to this simple and flavorful dish. Refrigerate leftover beef for sandwiches the next day or wrap in tortillas for Asian fajitas.

2	to 2½ pounds flank steak	1	tablespoon minced garlic
1	tablespoon baking soda	¼	cup hoisin sauce
2	tablespoons bourbon or whiskey	2	tablespoons vegetable oil
2	tablespoons sugar		

Trim all the fat from the flank steak.

In a large pan, put 4 cups cold water and the baking soda and stir to dissolve the baking soda. Place the flank steak in the pan and soak for 10 minutes. Remove the steak from the water and dry very well with paper towels.

In a bowl large enough to hold the steak, mix the bourbon, sugar, garlic, hoisin sauce, and vegetable oil very well and dip both sides of the steak in the mixture. Marinate on a plate for 2 to 3 hours or longer in the refrigerator.

Preheat the broiler or grill.

For medium doneness, broil for 4 to 5 minutes on each side, or until brown. If you want the meat to be well done, cook for 2 minutes longer. Remove from the broiler and let stand for 2 minutes. Slice across the grain into ¼-inch slices before serving.

basil beef

Frozen french fries can be used instead of fresh potatoes in this recipe, and we often have them on hand in our freezer. Fresh basil is necessary for bringing out the flavor of this beef dish.

10	ounces boneless beef sirloin	2	(6-ounce) all-purpose potatoes, cut into strips as for french fries (or use frozen french fries)
¼	teaspoon salt	2	tablespoons oyster sauce
¼	teaspoon white pepper	¼	teaspoon Tabasco sauce
1	teaspoon finely chopped fresh ginger	½	teaspoon sugar
1	teaspoon minced garlic	¼	cup sliced fresh basil leaves
2	teaspoons cornstarch		
3	tablespoons vegetable oil, divided		

Trim the fat from the beefsteak and cut the beef into 2 × ¼-inch strips (matchstick size).

In a bowl, combine the salt, pepper, ginger, garlic, and cornstarch. Add the beef and toss to combine.

Heat a large nonstick skillet over high heat. Add 2 tablespoons vegetable oil and the potato strips. Panfry fresh potatoes until slightly brown, 4 to 5 minutes. (If using frozen potatoes, it takes 2 to 3 minutes.) Remove and set aside.

Reheat the skillet over high heat and add the remaining 1 tablespoon oil and the beef. Stir-fry for 2 minutes, until the beef browns. Add the oyster sauce and cooked potatoes and stir-fry for 1 minute. Add the Tabasco sauce and sugar and stir well to combine. Turn off the heat, stir in the basil leaves, and serve.

beef tenderloin
with leek

Make sure to wash the leek thoroughly, as dirt gets trapped between the leaves. You may substitute onions, but leeks provide a truly interesting and unique flavor. Serve this over rice or noodles.

10	ounces beef tenderloin		1	small carrot, peeled
¼	teaspoon salt		2	tablespoons vegetable oil
	Dash white pepper		2	tablespoons oyster sauce
1	teaspoon cornstarch		½	teaspoon sugar
1	leek, white part only			

Trim the fat from the beefsteak and cut the beef into 2 × ¼-inch strips. In a medium bowl, toss the beef, salt, pepper, and cornstarch. Cover and refrigerate for 30 minutes.

Remove and discard the tough outer layers of the leek. Cut the leek in half lengthwise, wash very well to remove the sand, and drain well. Cut into ¼-inch slices crosswise. Cut the carrot into very thin strips, place in boiling water, and blanch for 1 minute. Drain, rinse with cold water, and drain well.

Heat a wok or nonstick skillet over high heat. Add the vegetable oil, beef, and leek and stir-fry for 1 minute, or until the meat browns. Add the carrot and stir-fry for 1 minute over high heat. Add the oyster sauce and the sugar and stir for 30 seconds.

beef with hot peppers

For a spicier version, experiment with different types of peppers like jalapeños or Thai chilies, both of which work well with the full flavor of beef. Serve over rice.

12 ounces sirloin or flank steak
¼   teaspoon salt
    Pinch white pepper
1   teaspoon cornstarch
1⅛ teaspoons sugar, divided

1   tablespoon vegetable oil
¼   cup thinly sliced shallots
1   teaspoon finely chopped fresh ginger
1   tablespoon brown bean paste
1   thinly sliced hot red chili pepper

Cut the beefsteak lengthwise into 2-inch strips. Cut the strips crosswise into ⅛-inch slices. In a bowl, toss the beef with the salt, pepper, cornstarch, and ⅛ teaspoon sugar.

Heat a wok or nonstick skillet over high heat and add the vegetable oil and beef. Stir until the beef turns brown, about 1 minute.

Add the shallots, ginger, brown bean paste, the remaining 1 teaspoon sugar, and the chili pepper and stir-fry for 1 minute.

braised beef shank

This can also be a wonderful appetizer in the summertime when served with marinated vegetables. You may freeze and reheat it for a quick lunch or dinner.

3	tablespoons vegetable oil	½	cup soy sauce
4	pounds whole beef shank (order from butcher)	2	teaspoons sugar
2	teaspoons finely chopped fresh ginger	4	whole star anise cloves
2	teaspoons minced garlic	½	cup Shaoxing rice wine or dry white wine

Heat a Dutch oven or large covered casserole over high heat. Add the oil, beef, ginger, and garlic. Turn and brown the entire beef shank, about 10 minutes in all.

Add the soy sauce and turn to coat the beef. Add the sugar, star anise, wine, and 1 cup water. Bring to a boil and boil for 5 minutes. Reduce the heat to low, cover, and cook for 3 hours.

After 3 hours, all the liquid should be absorbed. If more than ¼ cup of liquid remains, cook over high heat, uncovered, until the liquid is absorbed. Let cool slightly and cut crosswise into thin slices. Serve hot or cold.

braised chuck roast with daikon radish

Daikon radish can be found at Asian markets or some large grocery stores. If it is unavailable, use small white radishes instead. This is very good over fresh rice noodles.

1	(2½- to 3-pound) boned beef chuck roast (about 2 inches thick)	½	cup Shaoxing rice wine or red or white wine
1	teaspoon salt	6	whole star anise cloves
¼	teaspoon white pepper	1	tablespoon sugar
4	tablespoons cornstarch, divided	2	tablespoons vegetable oil
1	pound daikon radish	4	(¼-inch) fresh ginger slices
2	tablespoons dark soy sauce	2	teaspoons minced garlic
		½	teaspoon shredded green onion

Trim the fat from the chuck roast. Rub the chuck roast with the salt, pepper, and 2 tablespoons cornstarch.

Peel the daikon radish and cut into ½-inch slices.

In a small bowl, mix together the dark soy sauce, wine, star anise, and sugar. Set aside. In a small bowl, mix the remaining 2 tablespoons cornstarch with 2 tablespoons water and set aside.

Heat a wok or Dutch oven over high heat and add the vegetable oil, ginger, garlic, and chuck roast. Panfry the chuck roast to brown on both sides, about 2 minutes per side. Add the soy sauce mixture and cook for 1 minute, turning the beef 2 to 3 times. Add 2 cups water and bring to a boil. Cover and cook about 2 hours over medium-high heat, or until the sauce cooks down to about 2 cups liquid.

Add the daikon slices to the sauce and cook for 20 minutes over high heat, uncovered. Remove the beef, let sit for 10 minutes, and cut into ½-inch slices. Place on a serving platter.

Remove the star anise and ginger slices from the sauce and discard. Stir in the cornstarch mixture and cook until the sauce thickens, about 2 minutes. Turn off the heat and pour the sauce over the beef. Garnish with green onion.

shredded beef with red jalapeño peppers

serves 2

You may marinate the beef in the refrigerator for 4 to 5 hours in advance. This dish can be served over noodles or rice. The actual stir-frying time is very fast, so make sure all the ingredients are cut up and ready to go.

8	ounces boneless sirloin or round steak	1	red bell pepper
2	tablespoons + 2 teaspoons vegetable oil, divided	1	jalapeño pepper
		½	teaspoon finely chopped fresh ginger
¼	teaspoon salt	1	teaspoon minced garlic
	Dash white pepper	2	tablespoons hoisin sauce
2	teaspoons cornstarch	¼	cup roasted peanuts

Trim the fat from the beefsteak and cut the beef with the grain into 2-inch pieces. Slice across the grain into ¼-inch slices. Stack the slices and cut into thin strips. In a medium bowl, toss the beef with 2 teaspoons vegetable oil, the salt, white pepper, and cornstarch. Cover and refrigerate for 30 minutes.

Core, seed, and cut the red bell pepper into thin strips. Cut the jalapeño pepper in half lengthwise, remove the seeds and membrane, and cut into very thin strips.

Heat a nonstick skillet over high heat. Add the remaining 2 tablespoons vegetable oil, the beef, ginger, and garlic and stir-fry for 1 minute. Add the red bell pepper and the jalapeño pepper and stir-fry for 1 minute. Add the hoisin sauce and stir over high heat for 30 seconds. Add the peanuts and mix well.

steak, mongolian style

Red peppers were abundant in Mongolia, where spicy food was comforting during the harsh winters. Warm your family during the wintertime with this flavorful dish fit for a warrior-size appetite, accompanied by stir-fried vegetables and rice.

marinade

2	tablespoons brown bean paste		1	teaspoon sugar
2	tablespoons minced garlic		1	teaspoon black pepper
2	teaspoons finely chopped fresh ginger		2	teaspoons vegetable oil
1	teaspoon wine			
			4	(8-ounce) New York strip steaks

To make the marinade, in a small bowl, combine the brown bean paste, garlic, ginger, wine, sugar, black pepper, and vegetable oil and spread all over the steaks. Marinate for 1 hour, covered, in the refrigerator.

Preheat the broiler.

Broil the steaks for about 2 minutes on each side. Cut the steaks into ¼-inch slices and serve.

stir-fried beef with brussels sprouts

serves 2

Keep frozen brussels sprouts on hand for this quick and easy dinner. Serve with rice or noodles.

8	ounces boneless sirloin or flank steak		8	ounces brussels sprouts
2	tablespoons + 2 teaspoons vegetable oil, divided		½	teaspoon finely chopped fresh ginger
			1	teaspoon minced garlic
¼	teaspoon salt		1	jalapeño pepper, seeded and thinly sliced
	Dash white pepper		2	tablespoons hoisin sauce
2	teaspoons cornstarch		¼	cup roasted peanuts

Trim the fat from the beefsteak and cut the beef lengthwise into 2-inch strips. Cut the strips crosswise into ¼-inch slices. In a medium bowl, toss the beef with 2 teaspoons vegetable oil, the salt, white pepper, and cornstarch. Cover and refrigerate for 30 minutes.

Cut the ends from the brussels sprouts. Cut the brussels sprouts in half. Remove any dry or tough outside leaves. In a medium saucepan, heat 2 cups water to a boil. Place the brussels sprouts in the boiling water and blanch for 1 minute. Drain and rinse with cold water, drain very well, and set aside.

Heat a wok or nonstick skillet over high heat. Add the remaining 2 tablespoons vegetable oil, the beef, ginger, and garlic and stir-fry for 1 to 2 minutes. Add the brussels sprouts and jalapeño pepper and stir-fry for 1 minute. Add the hoisin sauce and stir over high heat for 30 seconds. Add the peanuts and mix well.

stir-fried beef with tomato and basil

This recipe has a unique flavor and goes well served over fresh rice or noodles.

10	ounces beef tenderloin	1	small white onion
4	teaspoons cornstarch, divided	2	medium tomatoes
5	teaspoons vegetable oil, divided	½	ounce (about 12 leaves) fresh basil
¼	teaspoon salt	1	teaspoon minced garlic
	Dash white pepper	2	tablespoons hoisin sauce

Trim the fat from the beefsteak and cut the beef lengthwise into 2-inch strips. Cut the strips crosswise into ¼-inch slices. In a medium bowl, toss the beef with 2 teaspoons cornstarch, 1 teaspoon vegetable oil, the salt, and pepper. Cover and refrigerate for 30 minutes.

Cut the onion into 1-inch squares. Cut the tomatoes into 8 wedges. Wash the basil and pat dry. In a small bowl, combine the remaining 2 teaspoons cornstarch and 1 tablespoon water and set aside.

Heat a nonstick skillet over high heat. Add the remaining 4 teaspoons vegetable oil, the beef, garlic, and onion and stir-fry for 1 minute, or until the meat browns. Continue stirring for about 2 minutes over high heat. Stir in the hoisin sauce and cornstarch mixture. As the mixture begins to thicken, after about 1 minute, add the tomatoes and basil; stir for 1 minute.

Pork

barbecued pork with five-spice powder

Five-spice powder is a common seasoning used in Chinese cuisine because of its unique intermingling of flavors. You can find five-spice powder at most grocery stores. Serve warm or cold with hot mustard or sweet-and-sour sauce (page 142), if desired.

Slice any leftover pork for sandwiches or dice for fried rice, salads, or noodles.

3   pounds fresh pork tenderloin (about 3)

marinade

½   cup ketchup
2   tablespoons sugar
1   tablespoon hoisin sauce
2   tablespoons white wine
2   teaspoons salt

1   tablespoon minced garlic
1   teaspoon five-spice powder

½   cup honey

Place the pork tenderloins in a large bowl. In a small bowl, mix together the ketchup, sugar, hoisin sauce, white wine, salt, garlic, and five-spice powder and pour over the pork. Turn the pork to coat with the marinade. Cover and refrigerate at least 1 hour or overnight.

Heat the oven to 450°F.

Place the pork on a rack in a roasting pan. Bake, uncovered, for 30 minutes. Reduce the oven temperature to 375°F. Turn the pork over and bake an additional 20 minutes, to an internal temperature of 170°F. Remove from the baking pan.

Brush the honey over the pork and cut on the diagonal into ¼-inch-thick slices.

ground pork with tofu

This is a delicious and easy recipe. Children love this dish served over hot, steaming rice—just omit the chili powder and cayenne. Add more spices if you want a spicier version (as it's usually prepared in China). You may also substitute ground chicken or turkey if you prefer.

14	ounces firm tofu		2	tablespoons brown bean paste
8	ounces ground pork		2	teaspoons chili powder
¼	teaspoon salt		2	teaspoons minced garlic
⅛	teaspoon white pepper		1	tablespoon hoisin sauce
1	teaspoon cornstarch		1	teaspoon sugar
2	tablespoons vegetable oil		1	teaspoon cayenne
1	teaspoon soy sauce		2	green onions, chopped

Cut the tofu into 8 squares (about 1½ inch square by ¾ inch thick). Set the tofu squares on a dishcloth to drain out any excess water.

In a bowl, mix the ground pork with the salt, pepper, and cornstarch.

Heat a wok or nonstick skillet over high heat and add the vegetable oil. Add the tofu and stir-fry until light brown, about 3 minutes. Add the soy sauce and continue to stir-fry for 30 seconds. Remove the tofu and reheat the wok. Add the ground pork and stir-fry until the pork turns white, about 2 minutes. Add the brown bean paste, chili powder, garlic, hoisin sauce, sugar, and cayenne. Stir-fry for 30 seconds and add the tofu to the pork mixture. Cook for 1 more minute. Remove to a serving platter and garnish with green onions.

honey barbecued pork

This is a simple recipe, although you must allow at least 2 hours for marinating. Marinate the pork in the refrigerator the night before, then just pop it in the oven for a super-quick dinner. Create a Chinatown rice bowl treat by slicing the pork and serving it over piping, hot rice, drizzled with oyster sauce.

3   pounds boneless pork butt or shoulder

marinade

¼   cup ketchup
2   teaspoons salt
4   teaspoons sugar
2   teaspoons minced garlic

2   teaspoons brandy
1   teaspoon five-spice powder
½   cup honey

Trim all the fat off the pork and cut the pork into six 1-inch-thick slices. In a small bowl, combine the ketchup, salt, sugar, garlic, brandy, five-spice powder, and honey. Rub this mixture on the pork pieces, covering all sides. Marinate the pork in the refrigerator, covered, for 2 hours or longer.

Heat the oven to 425°F.

Place the pork on a rack in a roasting pan and cook for 20 minutes. Turn the pork and cook for an additional 20 minutes. Reduce the heat to 350°F. and cook for an additional 20 minutes, until the pork reaches an internal temperature of 170°F. Remove from the oven. Brush any cooking sauce over the sliced pork before serving.

hot-and-sour pork with celery

This is a good dish to serve in the summer. You can also substitute chicken for the pork. This dish goes well with Noodles with Peanut Sauce (page 168).

8	ounces pork tenderloin	1	tablespoon vegetable oil
½	teaspoon salt, divided	2	teaspoons minced garlic
	Pinch white pepper	2	teaspoons white vinegar
1	teaspoon cornstarch	1	teaspoon sugar
1	hot red chili pepper	1	teaspoon light soy sauce
8	celery stalks	2	teaspoons sesame oil

Cut the pork into thin matchstick strips, 2 × ⅛ × ⅛ inch, and toss in a bowl with ¼ teaspoon salt, the pepper, and cornstarch.

Cut open the chili pepper and remove the seeds, then cut into thin 2-inch strips.

Remove and discard the celery leaves and the stringy stalks. Cut the stalks into 2 × ¼-inch slices.

Heat a wok or skillet over high heat and add the vegetable oil, garlic, celery, and remaining ¼ teaspoon salt. Stir-fry for 30 seconds and add the marinated pork strips. Turn the heat down to medium and stir-fry for an additional 2 minutes. Add the vinegar, sugar, soy sauce, sesame oil, and chili pepper and stir-fry over high heat for 1 more minute. Serve hot or cold.

pork medallions with peking sauce

Red pepper sauce adds a distinct spicy flavor to pork medallions and is a favorite preparation among the people of Beijing (formerly known as Peking).

10	ounces pork tenderloin
¼	teaspoon salt
⅛	teaspoon white pepper
2	tablespoons cornstarch
1	tablespoon vegetable oil
1	small tomato, thinly sliced
	Cilantro leaves, for garnish

sauce

¼	cup vinegar
¼	cup Chicken Broth (page 52)
2	tablespoons sugar
3	Thai red or green peppers, seeded and minced
2	teaspoons minced garlic
2	tablespoons cornstarch
2	tablespoons ketchup
⅛	teaspoon soy sauce

Cut the pork tenderloin crosswise into ½-inch slices. Sprinkle with the salt and white pepper. Flatten the pork by pressing down with your knife or hand and dust with 2 tablespoons cornstarch.

To make the sauce, in a small saucepan, combine the vinegar, chicken broth, and sugar. Bring to a boil over high heat. Stir in the Thai peppers and garlic. Combine the cornstarch with 2 tablespoons water and stir into the vinegar mixture until thickened, about 2 minutes. Stir in the ketchup and soy sauce. Set aside.

Heat a nonstick skillet over high heat and add the vegetable oil. Panfry both sides of the pork until brown, about 2 minutes on each side. Add the sauce and cook about 1 minute.

Arrange the pork in 2 rows on a platter, overlapping each piece slightly. Garnish with the tomato slices around the edge of the platter and place the cilantro leaves in the center.

pork tenderloin with wild mushrooms

You can experiment with a variety of mushrooms for this dish. You can also add other vegetables, such as asparagus, if you wish. Serve over rice.

10	ounces pork tenderloin	1	teaspoon minced garlic
¾	teaspoon salt, divided	¼	cup Chicken Broth (page 52)
¼	teaspoon white pepper	2	ounces shiitake mushrooms
2	tablespoons cornstarch	2	ounces oyster mushrooms
3	to 4 celery stalks	2	tablespoons oyster sauce
3	tablespoons vegetable oil, divided	3	green onions, with tops, chopped

Trim the silver skin from the pork tenderloin. Slice across the tenderloin into ½-inch pieces. Dust with ½ teaspoon salt and the pepper. Place the cornstarch on a plate or wax paper. Dip each piece of tenderloin in cornstarch to coat. Cut the celery into ¼-inch diagonal slices.

Heat a skillet or wok over high heat. Add 2 tablespoons vegetable oil and place the pork slices in a single layer, not overlapping. (If the skillet is not large enough, cook the pork in batches.) Fry until golden brown, turn over, and brown the other side, about 2 minutes per side. Reduce the heat and remove the pork from the skillet. Add the garlic, celery, and the remaining ¼ teaspoon salt to the skillet and stir-fry for 30 seconds. Add the chicken broth and cook for 3 minutes (the celery should absorb the broth). Add the mushrooms and the remaining 1 tablespoon vegetable oil and stir-fry for 1 minute. Add the oyster sauce, pork, and green onions and carefully stir for about 30 seconds. Remove to a serving platter.

sichuan ribs

You can deep-fry the ribs ahead of time and freeze them for later use. Simply refry and continue the preparation for dinner on the run or a quick solution to a potluck lunch with friends.

1	pound riblets (or have the butcher cut ribs into 2-inch sections)	2	tablespoons ketchup
½	teaspoon salt	1	teaspoon sugar
⅛	teaspoon white pepper	3	cups vegetable oil
2	tablespoons cornstarch	2	teaspoons minced garlic
1	tablespoon chili paste	2	tablespoons Chicken Broth (page 52)
		1	green onion, with tops, finely chopped

Trim the fat and remove the membrane from the ribs. Place the ribs in a shallow pan. Sprinkle all over with the salt, pepper, and cornstarch. Let sit for 30 minutes or longer (if marinating the ribs longer than 30 minutes, cover and place in the refrigerator).

In a small bowl, mix together the chili paste, ketchup, and sugar and set aside.

Heat the oil in a wok or large skillet to 350°F. Carefully place the coated ribs in the hot oil and deep-fry, stirring to separate the ribs. Turn the ribs over and continue to cook until the ribs turn brown, 3 to 4 minutes. Remove the ribs from the oil and carefully pour the oil from the wok or skillet, leaving 2 tablespoons in the bottom of the pan. Turn the heat to medium and add the ribs back to the pan. Add the garlic, chili paste mixture, and chicken broth and continue to cook until the ribs absorb most of the sauce, about 2 minutes. Place on a serving platter, garnish with the green onion, and serve immediately.

sizzling garlic pork

This fragrant dish is always a crowd pleaser at dinner parties. The sizzling sound always draws "oohs" and "ahhs" from guests and makes for a lively and fun presentation.

8 ounces pork tenderloin	½ cup Chicken Broth (page 52)
¼ teaspoon salt	1 tablespoon vegetable oil
⅛ teaspoon white pepper	2 teaspoons minced garlic
2 teaspoons cornstarch, divided	2½ cups thinly sliced celery
2 tablespoons brown bean paste	4 ounces shiitake mushrooms, thinly sliced
1¼ teaspoons sugar, divided	1 hot red chili pepper, seeded and thinly seeded
1 teaspoon white wine	2 green onions, cut into 1-inch pieces

Preheat the oven to 400°F. Place a 2-quart ovenproof heavy metal serving platter with deep edges in the oven to heat.

Cut the pork into 2 × 1 × ⅛-inch slices. Toss the pork with the salt, pepper, and 1 teaspoon cornstarch.

In a small bowl, mix the brown bean paste with 1 teaspoon sugar and the wine.

In a small bowl, combine the chicken broth, the remaining 1 teaspoon cornstarch, and the remaining ¼ teaspoon sugar and set aside.

Heat a wok or large nonstick skillet over high heat. Add the vegetable oil, garlic, and pork. Stir-fry for 1 minute and add the celery and mushrooms. Continue stirring 2 more minutes. Add the bean paste mixture and chili pepper. Stir and continue cooking until the pork is done, about 1 minute. Add the cornstarch mixture and cook about 1 minute, or until thickened. Remove from the heat (see Note) and add the green onions. Pour into the preheated sizzling platter just before you serve for a special presentation.

NOTE: If you won't be serving this pork recipe on a special preheated metal platter, cook for an additional 30 seconds after adding the green onions.

stir-fried pork with asian eggplant

Asian eggplant, usually called Japanese eggplant, can be found at Asian markets and some grocery stores. With its firm texture and few seeds, it is preferred for Chinese cooking. Larger purple eggplants may be used instead if it is not available; just cut the eggplants into 1/2-inch cubes.

8	ounces pork loin or pork tenderloin	1	teaspoon sugar
1¼	teaspoons salt, divided	1	teaspoon white wine
	Pinch white pepper	2	tablespoons vegetable oil
2	teaspoons cornstarch	2	teaspoons minced garlic
3	Japanese eggplants	¼	cup Chicken Broth (page 52)
2	green onions	2	medium jalapeño peppers, seeded and thinly sliced
2	tablespoons brown bean paste		

Cut the pork into 2 × 1 × ⅛-inch slices. Toss the pork slices with ¼ teaspoon salt, the white pepper, and cornstarch.

Wash the eggplants. Cut off the ends of the eggplants and discard. Cut the eggplants lengthwise in half, then slice diagonally into ½-inch pieces. Sprinkle the remaining 1 teaspoon salt over the eggplants and cover with cold water. Stir and let soak for 10 minutes. Drain and pat dry with paper towels. Cut the green onions into 1-inch pieces. In a small bowl, mix together the brown bean paste, sugar, and white wine and set aside.

Heat a wok or large nonstick skillet over high heat. Add the vegetable oil, garlic, pork, and eggplants and stir-fry for 3 minutes. Stir in the bean paste mixture, mix well, and add the chicken broth. Continue to cook until the liquid is absorbed, about 2 minutes. Add the jalapeño peppers and green onions and stir for an additional 30 seconds. Remove to a platter and serve.

stir-fried pork with bean sprouts

serves 4

This recipe only takes 5 minutes to cook and goes well over fresh noodles or rice.

8	ounces pork loin	2	tablespoons vegetable oil
½	teaspoon salt, divided	1	teaspoon minced garlic
	Dash white pepper	2	hot red chili peppers, seeded and thinly sliced
1	teaspoon cornstarch		into strips
1	leek	1	tablespoon oyster sauce
8	ounces bean sprouts		

Cut the pork into 2-inch-long matchstick pieces. Toss the pork with ¼ teaspoon salt, the white pepper, and cornstarch.

Cut off the end of the leek and discard the tough leaves. Wash the leek well, separating the layers, and dry. Using the white and light green parts only, cut across the leek into ¼-inch strips. Rinse the bean sprouts with cold water and drain well. Set aside.

Heat a wok or large nonstick skillet over high heat. Add the vegetable oil, garlic, and pork and stir-fry for 1 minute. Add the bean sprouts, leek, remaining ¼ teaspoon salt, and the chili peppers. Continue to stir-fry for 2 minutes. Stir in the oyster sauce and mix well. Remove to a platter and serve.

stir-fried pork with zucchini

In China, cucumbers are used for this recipe—zucchini is not obtainable there. Smaller zucchini work best, but if they aren't available, cut the larger ones in half lengthwise before slicing. For a stronger flavor, add chili pepper with the garlic. This is definitely an easy and healthful recipe.

8	ounces pork loin or pork tenderloin			black mushrooms)
⅛	teaspoon salt		1	tablespoon oyster sauce
⅛	teaspoon white pepper		¼	teaspoon sugar
3	teaspoons cornstarch, divided		1	tablespoon vegetable oil
1	large zucchini (about 12 ounces) or		1	teaspoon minced garlic
	2 to 3 small zucchini		¼	cup Chicken Broth (page 52)
2	tablespoons dried cloud ears (or substitute			

Cut the pork into thin 2 × 1 × ⅛-inch slices. Toss the pork with the salt, pepper, and 1 teaspoon cornstarch.

Wash and dry the zucchini with paper towels. Cut off and discard the end. Slice diagonally into ¼-inch slices.

Soak the cloud ears in warm water until soft, about 20 minutes. Wash well to remove any sand. Drain well and pat dry on paper towels.

In a small bowl, combine the remaining 2 teaspoons cornstarch, 2 teaspoons water, the oyster sauce, and sugar. Stir well to mix thoroughly.

Heat a wok or skillet over high heat. Add the vegetable oil, garlic, and marinated pork and stir-fry for 30 seconds. Add the zucchini and cloud ears and stir-fry for 2 minutes.

Add the chicken broth and bring to a boil. Stir in the cornstarch mixture and cook until the sauce thickens, 1 to 2 minutes. Serve.

tofu with pork tenderloin in a clay pot

Clay pots found in Chinatown come in a variety of designs. You may also use an ovenproof casserole with a cover.

8	ounces pork tenderloin	1	teaspoon finely chopped fresh ginger
¼	teaspoon salt	1	teaspoon minced garlic
	Pinch white pepper	4	Thai red or green peppers, seeded and diced
1	tablespoon cornstarch	1	tablespoon dark soy sauce
7	dried black mushrooms	2	tablespoons hoisin sauce
14	ounces firm tofu	1	green onion, with top, chopped
2	tablespoons vegetable oil, divided		

Preheat the oven to 400°F. Place a 2-quart clay pot or heavy casserole with a cover into the oven to heat.

Cut the pork tenderloin into ½-inch slices. In a small bowl, combine the salt, white pepper, and cornstarch. Coat the pork pieces with the cornstarch mixture and set aside.

Soak the black mushrooms in hot water until soft, about 20 minutes; drain. Rinse in cold water; drain. Remove and discard the stems and cut the caps into ½-inch strips.

Cut the tofu into ¾-inch cubes.

Heat a nonstick wok or skillet over high heat. Add 1 tablespoon vegetable oil, the pork, ginger, garlic, Thai peppers, and black mushrooms; stir and separate the pork for 1 minute. Stir in the soy sauce and hoisin sauce. Mix well and turn off the heat.

Remove the clay pot from the oven. Add the remaining 1 tablespoon vegetable oil, the tofu, and green onion to the clay pot. Pour the pork mixture on top of the tofu. Cover and place in the oven for 15 to 20 minutes. Stir before serving.

To hold longer than 30 minutes, turn the oven off and keep warm until ready to serve.

seafood

Asparagus Wrapped with Shrimp and Tofu

Crispy Fish with Ginger-Scallion Sauce

Braided Fish Steamed with Ginger and Green Onions

Chow Shung Ding

Crispy Scallops with Garlic Sauce

Golden Stuffed Tofu with Shrimp

Jade Shrimp with Fragrant Vegetables

Lobster with Ginger and Scallions

Mussels with Cilantro Sauce

Panfried Sea Bass

Panfried Shrimp with Spicy Sauce

Poached Shrimp with Wine

Salmon Steak

Salmon with Tofu

Seafood Tofu Dumplings with Broccoli

Steamed Fish Fillets

Steamed Tofu with Sun-Dried Scallops

Steamed Whole Fish

Stir-Fried Seafood with Snow Peas

Stuffed Eggplant with Shrimp and Tofu

Sweet-and-Sour Fish

Tea-Smoked Sea Bass

Tofu Crabmeat Medallions

Walnut Shrimp

asparagus wrapped with
shrimp and tofu

This can be served as a colorful and healthy appetizer or a light entrée and it's a cinch to prepare ahead of time. Store in the refrigerator up to 12 hours in advance before panfrying. To keep the fat count down, use vegetable oil spray on a nonstick skillet instead of adding oil to the pan.

1¼	teaspoons salt, divided	3	ounces firm tofu
10	ounces shrimp, shelled and deveined	½	teaspoon minced garlic
2	ounces drained canned water chestnuts	16	asparagus spears
1	large shallot	2	tablespoons bread crumbs
1	small egg white	2	tablespoons cornstarch
	Pinch white pepper	2	tablespoons vegetable oil
1	tablespoon cornstarch	¼	cup Chicken Broth (page 52)

Fill a bowl with warm water and add 1 teaspoon salt; stir to dissolve. Place the shrimp in the salt water and swirl. Leave the shrimp in the salt water for 5 minutes, then rinse with cold water and drain. Pat dry on paper towels.

In a food processor, finely chop the water chestnuts and shallot. Add the egg white, shrimp, remaining ¼ teaspoon salt, the pepper, cornstarch, tofu, and garlic and mix to a paste.

Wash the asparagus and drain. Break off and discard the thick tough ends. Cut the asparagus into 4-inch pieces.

In a small bowl, combine the bread crumbs and cornstarch. Evenly spread the mixture on a piece of wax paper.

Take 2 tablespoons of the shrimp mixture and place on the bread crumb and cornstarch mixture. Set 2 pieces of asparagus on top of the shrimp mixture. Pull the shrimp mixture from the sides to cover the asparagus. Roll lightly in the bread crumb and cornstarch mixture. Continue the process until all the mixtures are used up.

Heat a nonstick skillet over medium heat. Add the vegetable oil. Place the asparagus rolls in the pan ½ inch apart. Panfry over medium heat until golden brown, turning frequently, about 2 minutes in all.

Add the chicken broth and cook until fully absorbed, about 3 minutes. Serve hot.

crispy fish with ginger-scallion sauce

You may substitute sea bass for this recipe. This is an excellent dish for a dinner party or special occasion, particularly because it can be marinated the night before in the refrigerator. For variety, you may also prepare it with sweet-and-sour sauce (see page 142).

ginger-scallion sauce

2	tablespoons vegetable oil
2	teaspoons finely chopped fresh ginger
2	teaspoons minced garlic
½	cup Chicken Broth (page 52)
¼	cup vinegar
¼	cup soy sauce
1	tablespoon sugar
¼	cup chopped green onions

1½	pounds whole walleye or snapper, well cleaned
2⅛	teaspoons salt, divided
2	teaspoons finely chopped fresh ginger
⅛	teaspoon sugar
2	teaspoons sesame oil
2	green onions, sliced
¼	cup all-purpose flour
2	tablespoons cornstarch
¼	teaspoon baking soda
5	cups vegetable oil

To prepare the sauce, in a small saucepan over high heat, heat 2 tablespoons vegetable oil. Sauté 2 teaspoons ginger and the garlic. Add the chicken broth, vinegar, soy sauce, and sugar and bring to a boil. Remove from the heat and allow to cool. Add the chopped green onions when ready to serve.

Make 3 cuts across the fish almost down to the bone. In a small bowl, combine 2 teaspoons salt, 2 teaspoons ginger, ⅛ teaspoon sugar, and the sesame oil and rub the inside and outside of the fish. Marinate for 20 minutes (if longer, cover and refrigerate). Stuff the fish cavity with the sliced green onions and place on a baking sheet or platter.

In a small bowl, combine the flour, cornstarch, baking soda, ¼ cup water, ½ tablespoon oil, and the remaining ⅛ teaspoon salt. Mix into a smooth batter and brush over the fish.

Heat the vegetable oil to 375°F. in a wok or large, deep skillet. Deep-fry the fish until golden brown, 6 to 7 minutes. Drain well. Place on a platter. Serve with the ginger-scallion sauce on the side.

braided fish, steamed with ginger and green onions

This recipe requires a lot of trimming to make the long strips for braiding the fish, but the remaining fish can be used in another dish or a soup. This is a very impressive dish for guests with an interesting "twist." For a simpler preparation, skip the braiding and steam as directed. Also, you can use just one kind of fish for this recipe, but it won't be as visually interesting. Guests can take a little of each or select the fish they prefer.

1	skinless salmon fillet (about 2 pounds)	¼	teaspoon white pepper
1	skinless halibut fillet (about 2 pounds)	1	teaspoon garlic
1	tablespoon finely chopped fresh ginger, divided	1	tablespoon cornstarch
½	teaspoon salt	2	tablespoons soy sauce
½	teaspoon sugar	½	cup finely shredded green onions
¼	cup + 1 tablespoon vegetable oil, divided		

Cut the salmon into 3 long ¾-inch-wide strips (save the trimmings for another use). Cut the halibut into 2 long ¾-inch-wide strips and also save the extra for another use. In a small bowl, blend 2 teaspoons ginger, the salt, sugar, 1 tablespoon oil, the pepper, and garlic. Spread over the fish and marinate for ½ hour or longer, covered, in the refrigerator.

Sprinkle the cornstarch over the fish. Using 2 strips of salmon and 1 strip of halibut, braid into a straight, long braid. You will need to cut the third strip of salmon in half and use about half of the second halibut strip to continue the braid. Tuck the connecting edges in as best you can so it looks like a continuous braid. Place on a heatproof platter (see Note) and cover with heavy plastic wrap for 10 minutes (or longer if refrigerated).

Place the plate of braided fish on a rack in a steamer. Cover and steam over boiling water until the fish flakes easily with a fork, 10 to 15 minutes.

In a small saucepan, heat the remaining ¼ cup vegetable oil. Add the remaining 1 teaspoon ginger. When the ginger sizzles, pour the oil over the fish. Pour the soy sauce over the fish and garnish with the green onions.

NOTE: If you can't find halibut fillets, substitute orange roughy (you'd
need 2 fillets, or about 1 to 1¼ pounds).

This recipe can also be cooked in the microwave. Place the
braids on a plate, cover loosely with plastic wrap, and
microwave on high for 2 minutes. Let stand for 2 minutes.
Rotate the plate and microwave for an additional 3 minutes.

chow shung ding

serves 4

*"Shung Ding" literally means "both diced." If you have some cooked shrimp left over from dinner
the night before, simply follow the preparation, but add the cooked and diced shrimp pieces at the
end for a quick and easy family meal.*

1	teaspoon salt, divided	½	red bell pepper
½	pound medium shrimp, shelled and deveined	2	tablespoons vegetable oil
2	teaspoons cornstarch, divided	2	teaspoons minced garlic
¼	teaspoon white pepper	2	tablespoons hoisin sauce
¼	pound skinless, boneless chicken breast, cut into ¾-inch cubes	2	teaspoons chili paste
1	teaspoon finely chopped fresh ginger	½	cup canned water chestnuts, diced
½	green bell pepper	2	tablespoons chopped green onion, with tops

Place ½ teaspoon salt and 1 cup warm water in a small bowl and soak the shrimp for 5 minutes. Rinse with cold water and pat dry with paper towels. In a medium bowl, toss the shrimp,
1 teaspoon cornstarch, and the white pepper. Set aside. Toss the chicken with the ginger, the
remaining ½ teaspoon salt, and the remaining teaspoon cornstarch and set aside.

Cut the green and red bell peppers into ¾-inch pieces.

Heat a wok over high heat. Add the vegetable oil, garlic, chicken, and shrimp. Stir-fry for
1 minute, or until the shrimp turn pink. Stir in the hoisin sauce, chili paste, green and red peppers, and water chestnuts; stir-fry for 2 to 3 minutes. Place on a platter and garnish with the
green onion.

crispy scallops with garlic sauce

You may deep-fry the scallops ahead of time. Simply refry or reheat in the oven before serving.

1	pound sea scallops	1	tablespoon minced garlic
1¼	teaspoons salt, divided	¾	cup Chicken Broth (page 52)
¼	teaspoon white pepper	¾	cup white vinegar
1	teaspoon sesame oil	1	cup sugar
1	small egg white	½	cup all-purpose flour
¼	cup + 2 tablespoons cornstarch, divided	½	teaspoon baking soda
½	teaspoon dark soy sauce	2	green onions, diced
4	cups + 2 tablespoons vegetable oil, divided		

Remove the muscle on the outside of each scallop and rinse the scallops in cold water; drain thoroughly. Pat the scallops dry with paper towels. In a medium bowl, mix ½ teaspoon salt, the pepper, sesame oil, egg white, and 1 tablespoon cornstarch. Stir in the scallops, cover, and refrigerate for 30 minutes.

In a small bowl, mix together 1 tablespoon cornstarch, 1 tablespoon water, and the dark soy sauce and set aside. In a small saucepan over medium heat, heat 1 tablespoon vegetable oil and the garlic. Cook until the garlic is fragrant. Add the chicken broth, vinegar, sugar, and ¼ teaspoon salt and cook to boiling. Stir in the cornstarch mixture and return to boiling. Remove from the heat.

Heat 4 cups vegetable oil, 1½ inches deep, in a wok to 350°F. In a medium bowl, mix ½ cup water, the flour, the remaining ¼ cup cornstarch, the remaining 1 tablespoon vegetable oil, the baking soda, and the remaining ½ teaspoon salt. Stir the scallops into the batter until well coated. Fry 8 scallops at a time for 2 minutes, or until light brown, turning occasionally; drain on paper towels. Continue until all the scallops are cooked. The scallops can be cooked to this point ahead of time.

Increase the oil temperature to 375°F. Refry the scallops for about 1 minute, or until golden brown; drain on paper towels. Meanwhile, reheat the garlic sauce and gently mix with the scallops. Garnish with the diced green onions and serve immediately.

golden stuffed tofu
with shrimp

serves 4

Use a deep enough pan or wok to deep-fry—tofu contains a lot of water, and spattering can occur. We recommend frying 1 to 2 pieces at a time to maintain high heat. This dish is referred to as "Pile of Gold" and is often served for Chinese New Year banquets.

14	ounces firm tofu
2¼	teaspoons salt, divided
4	ounces shrimp, shelled and deveined
1	small egg white
	Dash white pepper
1	teaspoon sesame oil
1	teaspoon cornstarch

gravy

1	tablespoon cornstarch
1	cup Chicken Broth (page 52)
1	tablespoon oyster sauce
3	cups vegetable oil
2	tablespoons thinly sliced green onion

Cut the tofu into 8 squares about 1½ inches square by ¾ inch thick. Scoop the tofu out of the center of each square, making a box, and reserve the scooped-out tofu. Set the tofu squares upside down on a cloth to drain the excess water out.

Place 2 cups warm water in a bowl and add 2 teaspoons salt; stir to dissolve. Place the shrimp in the salt water and swirl. Leave the shrimp in the salt water for 5 minutes, then rinse with cold water and drain. Pat dry on paper towels to remove the excess water. Using a sharp knife or food processor, mash the shrimp to a paste. Blend with the egg white, the remaining ¼ teaspoon salt, pepper, sesame oil, and cornstarch.

With a fork, mash half of the scooped-out tofu and add to the shrimp mixture. Put about 1 teaspoon of the mixture in each square of tofu. Repeat until all 8 pieces are filled.

To prepare the gravy, in a small bowl, mix the cornstarch with 1 tablespoon cold water. In a small saucepan, bring the chicken broth and oyster sauce to a boil and add the cornstarch mixture. Stir until thickened, about 1 minute, and remove from the heat.

In a deep-sided pan (so the oil doesn't boil over from the excess moisture in the tofu), heat the vegetable oil to 350°F. Add one piece of tofu at a time to the hot oil to prevent them from sticking together. Do not overcrowd the pan. Deep-fry only 1 to 2 pieces at a time. Fry until golden brown, 2 to 3 minutes. Drain on paper towels when done.

Reheat the gravy and pour over the tofu. Garnish with the green onion and serve immediately.

jade shrimp with fragrant vegetables

serves 4

This recipe uses only the stems of the broccoli, so make this recipe when you have broccoli stems left over from another recipe. You'll need to buy 2 1/2 pounds of broccoli to end up with 1 pound of tender stem slices. To prepare this recipe using both stems and florets, you would only need to buy 1 pound of broccoli, cutting the florets 2 inches long.

2¼	teaspoons salt, divided	2	tablespoons oyster sauce
1	pound large shrimp, peeled and deveined	3	tablespoons vegetable oil, divided
4	teaspoons cornstarch, divided	1	teaspoon minced garlic
⅛	teaspoon white pepper	1	small white onion, thinly sliced
½	teaspoon sesame oil	½	cup Chicken Broth (page 52)
1	pound broccoli stems	2	ounces canned baby corn
4	ounces snow peas	¼	cup cilantro leaves, for garnish

Place 4 cups warm water in a bowl and add 2 teaspoons salt; stir to dissolve. Place the shrimp in the salt water and swirl. Leave the shrimp in the salt water for 5 minutes, then rinse with cold water and drain. Pat dry on paper towels.

In a medium bowl, toss the shrimp with 1 teaspoon cornstarch, the pepper, and sesame oil. Cover and set aside.

Cut the florets off the stems and save for another use. Cut off the end of the stem (about 1 inch). Peel the skin off each stalk and slice diagonally into ¼-inch slices. Remove the strings from the snow peas. In a saucepan, place 2 cups water and bring to a boil. Add the snow peas and return to boiling. Immediately drain and rinse with cold water until the snow peas are cold. Drain thoroughly. In a small bowl, mix 1 tablespoon water, the remaining 1 tablespoon cornstarch, and the oyster sauce. Set aside.

Heat a wok over high heat. Add 2 tablespoons vegetable oil, the garlic, and shrimp and stir-fry for 2 minutes, or until the shrimp turn pink. Remove from the wok and set aside. Reheat the wok over high heat. Add the remaining 1 tablespoon vegetable oil and tilt the wok to coat the sides. Add the broccoli stems and onion and stir-fry for 1 minute. Add the chicken broth and heat to boiling. Cover and cook for 1 minute. Stir in the cornstarch mixture and cook until thickened, about 1 minute. Add the baby corn and the remaining ¼ teaspoon salt and stir-fry for 1 minute. Add the shrimp and snow peas; cook and stir for 1 minute, until the shrimp are hot. Garnish with cilantro leaves and serve.

lobster with ginger and scallions

You can actually deep-fry the lobster and freeze it, then simply reheat the lobster in the oven, pre-
pare the sauce, and stir-fry them together. You may use frozen lobster tails (ask the butcher to chop
each tail into 6 pieces).

½	teaspoon salt
¼	teaspoon white pepper
½	cup + 1 tablespoon cornstarch, divided
1	live lobster (about 2 pounds)
3	cups + 2 tablespoons vegetable oil, divided

¼	cup finely chopped fresh ginger
4	green onions, cut into 1-inch pieces + ½ cup finely shredded green onions
1	cup Chicken Broth (page 52)

On a plate, combine the salt, pepper, and ½ cup cornstarch. In a small bowl, combine the remaining 1 tablespoon cornstarch and 1 tablespoon water; set aside.

In a large pot, place the lobster and cover with cold water (water should be 1 inch above the lobster). Remove the lobster and bring the water to a boil. Submerge the lobster in the boiling water and cook for 3 minutes. Remove from the water and twist off the head and cut off the end of the tail (clean the inside of the head and save it and the tail for garnish). Twist off and discard the legs. Cutting through the shell, slice the tail in half and cut across the tail twice, making 6 pieces. Cut the claws in half or use a hammer to crack them open. Coat all exposed lobster meat, including the claws, with the dry cornstarch mixture.

In a wok or large, deep skillet, heat 3 cups vegetable oil to 350°F. Deep-fry the lobster for 1 minute. Remove from the oil and drain. Remove the oil from the wok. Wash, dry, and reheat the wok over high heat. Add the remaining 2 tablespoons oil, the ginger, cut green onions, and lobster to the wok. Stir to mix. Add the chicken broth and bring to a boil. Stir in the cornstarch-water mixture and continue stirring until the sauce thickens, about 30 seconds.

Place on a serving platter and garnish with the shredded green onions. Place the cleaned lobster head at the top of the platter and the tail at the opposite end for garnish.

mussels with cilantro sauce

These mussels would also be excellent with ¼ cup packaged black bean sauce for noncilantro lovers. This dish goes well with Yeung Chau Fried Rice (page 177).

1	pound mussels	½	cup red wine
¼	cup + 1 tablespoon vegetable oil, divided	2	tablespoons oyster sauce
3	teaspoons minced garlic, divided	¼	cup finely chopped fresh cilantro leaves

Brush the mussels very well under cold running water; drain well.

In a saucepan, heat 1 tablespoon vegetable oil. Add 2 teaspoons garlic and the mussels and cook for 30 seconds. Add the red wine and ½ cup water, cover, and cook for 1 minute, or until the mussels are all open (discard the ones that stay closed). Remove the mussels with a slotted spoon. Remove the top half of each shell, leaving the mussels intact on the bottom half of the shell. Arrange the mussels on a serving platter.

Heat a wok or large skillet over medium heat. Add the remaining ¼ cup vegetable oil and the remaining 1 teaspoon garlic and cook until the garlic becomes fragrant. Turn off the heat and stir in the oyster sauce and chopped cilantro, mixing well. Spoon the sauce over the cooked mussels and serve.

panfried sea bass

Pair this dish with a light vegetable stir-fry for a fast but excellent dinner. You may substitute halibut or walleye. Low-fat tip: Use a nonstick pan and vegetable oil spray.

8	ounces skinless sea bass fillet		2	teaspoons hoisin sauce
½	teaspoon salt		1	teaspoon brown bean sauce
	Pinch white pepper		1	green onion
1	teaspoon finely chopped fresh ginger		1	tablespoon vegetable oil
1	teaspoon minced garlic			

Sprinkle the sea bass with salt, pepper, ginger, and garlic and marinate for 30 minutes or longer in the refrigerator.

In a small bowl, mix the hoisin and brown bean sauces together well.

Cut the green onion into 2-inch pieces, place in a small bowl, and set aside.

Heat a skillet or wok over high heat. Add the vegetable oil and sea bass and panfry until both sides are browned, about 2 minutes per side. Reduce the heat to medium. Brush half of the hoisin/brown bean sauce mixture on one side of the sea bass. Turn the sea bass over and brush the remaining sauce mixture on the other side. Turn over again and cook an additional minute, 6 minutes in all. Remove from the pan, garnish with the green onion, and serve immediately.

panfried shrimp with spicy sauce

Soaking the shrimp in salt water draws out any impurities. Make sure to rinse the shrimp thoroughly. Once the shrimp have been cleaned, you may store them in the refrigerator up to 24 hours before cooking. This is a fun dish to eat with your hands. Have colorful water bowls handy for your guests to dip their sticky fingers in.

1	pound medium shrimp (in the shell, about 20)	1	teaspoon sugar
1	tablespoon salt	1	tablespoon light soy sauce
2	green onions, with tops	2	teaspoons chili paste
¼	cup ketchup	2	teaspoons minced garlic
1	tablespoon white wine	3	tablespoons vegetable oil

With scissors, remove the legs from the shrimp. Leaving the shell intact ¼ inch at each end, cut each shell lengthwise ½ inch down the back with a small knife. Remove and discard the sand vein.

In a medium bowl, place 2 cups water and the salt; stir until the salt dissolves. Add the shrimp and let sit for 5 minutes. Remove the shrimp from the salt water and rinse well with cold water. Drain in a colander and pat dry with paper towels.

Cut the green onions into 2-inch pieces.

In a small bowl, combine the ketchup, wine, sugar, soy sauce, chili paste, and garlic.

Heat a skillet or wok over high heat. Add the vegetable oil; rotate the pan to coat the sides. Place the shrimp in a single layer in the wok (do not overlap). Fry the shrimp until pink, turning once, about 3 minutes. Stir in the ketchup mixture and stir-fry over high heat for approximately 1 minute. Add the green onions and cook and stir for 30 seconds. Serve hot or cold, as an entrée or appetizer.

poached shrimp with wine

You may make these shrimp with water instead of wine. This dish also may be served as an appetizer. A salad or vegetable stir-fry will complete a light meal.

1	pound shrimp (in the shell, about 20)
2	teaspoons salt
2	cups white wine or rice wine

dipping sauce

¼	cup light soy sauce
¼	cup sugar
½	teaspoon minced garlic
1	teaspoon sesame oil

Leaving the shell of the shrimp intact, cut the shell lengthwise down the back with scissors or a very sharp knife. Remove and discard the sand vein.

In a medium bowl, place 2 cups warm water and add the salt; stir to dissolve. Place the shrimp in the salt water and swirl. Leave the shrimp in the salt water for 5 minutes, then rinse with cold water and drain. Pat dry on paper towels.

In a saucepan, place the shrimp and wine and bring to a boil. Cover, turn off the heat, and let sit for 2 minutes.

Remove the shrimp to serve. Save the wine for another use.

In a small bowl, combine the soy sauce, sugar, garlic, and sesame oil and stir well. Serve with the shrimp.

salmon steak

This recipe is a very fast dinner when you serve it with your favorite salad or steamed vegetables. The whole recipe takes only 10 to 15 minutes from start to finish.

3	salmon steaks (about 1½ pounds total)	2	teaspoons soy sauce
⅛	teaspoon salt	2	tablespoons dry white wine
⅛	teaspoon white pepper	1	teaspoon sugar
1	tablespoon vegetable oil	4	green onions, with tops, cut into 1-inch pieces
1	teaspoon finely chopped fresh ginger		

Rinse the salmon steaks with cold water. Pat dry with paper towels and sprinkle the salmon steaks with the salt and pepper.

Heat a wok or skillet over high heat. Add the vegetable oil, ginger, and salmon steaks. Panfry for 1 minute on each side, or until light brown; add the soy sauce. Turn the steaks over to coat with the soy sauce and then add the wine and sugar. Turn the steaks over again so the sauce completely coats them. Reduce the heat and add the green onions. Cook for 1 minute over medium heat. Serve immediately.

salmon with tofu

This dish is very high in protein and is very simple to make. We prefer a nonstick skillet for this dish. Serve with hot, steaming rice. Add 2 tablespoons of hot chili pepper along with the garlic when sautéing the salmon for a spicy version of this recipe.

10	ounces skinless salmon fillet
1	teaspoon finely chopped fresh ginger
⅛	teaspoon salt
⅛	teaspoon white pepper
3	teaspoons cornstarch, divided
14	ounces firm tofu
1	tablespoon soy sauce

1	tablespoon hoisin sauce
½	cup Chicken Broth (page 52)
1	tablespoon vegetable oil
1	teaspoon minced garlic
¼	cup fresh or frozen peas
¼	cup chopped green onions

Cut the salmon fillet into ¾-inch chunks. In a medium bowl, mix with the ginger, salt, pepper, and 1 teaspoon cornstarch.

Cut the tofu into ½-inch diced pieces. Place on a paper towel to absorb the water and set aside.

In a small bowl, mix the soy sauce and hoisin sauce.

In a small bowl, mix the chicken broth with the remaining 2 teaspoons cornstarch and set aside.

Heat a wok or skillet until hot. Add the vegetable oil, garlic, salmon, and tofu. Stir-fry for about 1 minute. Add the peas and soy sauce mixture. Continue to stir for 2 minutes. Stir in the chicken broth mixture and cook until the sauce thickens, about 1 minute.

Add the green onions and stir for 10 seconds. Remove from the pan and serve immediately.

seafood tofu dumplings with broccoli

serves 4 to 6

This dish is extremely versatile. You may deep-fry the dumplings ahead of time and use virtually any type of vegetable. Sometimes we skip the vegetables and eat the deep-fried dumplings alone with sauce as an appetizer.

2	teaspoons salt, divided	¼	teaspoon white pepper
½	pound shrimp, peeled and deveined	1	egg
½	pound skinless fish fillets (such as salmon, walleye, sea bass, or other)	2	tablespoons oyster sauce
		1	teaspoon sugar
10	ounces firm tofu	1	pound broccoli florets
¼	cup chopped green onions, with tops	4	cups vegetable oil
5	tablespoons cornstarch, divided	2	cups Chicken Broth (page 52)
1	teaspoon sesame oil		

In a medium bowl, place 2 cups warm water and add 1 teaspoon salt; stir to dissolve. Place the shrimp in the salt water and swirl. Leave the shrimp in the salt water for 5 minutes, then rinse with cold water and drain. Pat dry on paper towels. Using a sharp knife or a food processor, chop the shrimp finely.

Rinse the fish fillets with cold water and pat dry. Finely mince the fish.

In a medium bowl, mash the tofu with a fork. Stir in the shrimp, fish, green onions, 2 tablespoons cornstarch, the sesame oil, the remaining 1 teaspoon salt, the pepper, and egg with a fork until well mixed.

In a small bowl, combine the oyster sauce, the remaining 3 tablespoons cornstarch, 3 tablespoons water, and the sugar and set aside.

Bring a saucepan of water to a boil. Place the broccoli in the boiling water for 2 minutes. Drain and arrange the broccoli on the edge of a serving platter.

In a wok or large, deep skillet, heat the oil to 350°F. Using a spoon large enough to hold 1 tablespoon of the tofu mixture, use another large spoon to push the mixture into the oil, forming an egg-shaped dumpling. After 1 minute, turn the dumpling and cook the other side for another minute until golden brown. Remove from the oil and drain on paper towels. Repeat until the entire mixture is cooked.

In a 2-quart saucepan, bring the chicken broth to a boil. Stir in the cornstarch mixture until thickened, about 1 minute.

Place the dumplings in the center of the platter, pour the sauce over the dumplings, and serve.

steamed fish fillets

serves 4

In Chinese homes, this recipe is often prepared for everyday dinners. While the fish is steaming, you can stir-fry vegetables for a healthy, simple meal.

1	pound skinless halibut, salmon, or sea bass fillets	1	teaspoon cornstarch
1	tablespoon finely chopped fresh ginger	2	green onions
½	teaspoon salt	3	tablespoons vegetable oil
⅛	teaspoon white pepper	1	teaspoon minced garlic
1	teaspoon sesame oil	3	tablespoons soy sauce

Pat the fish fillets dry with paper towels. In a small bowl, blend the ginger, salt, pepper, and sesame oil together. Spread over the fish and marinate for ½ hour or longer in the refrigerator.

Coat the fish with the cornstarch.

Cut the green onions into 2-inch pieces, then shred into thin strips. Soak in a bowl of ice water for 10 minutes, drain, and set aside for the garnish.

Place the fish fillets on a heatproof plate and place on a rack in a steamer (see Note). Cover and steam over boiling water until the fish flakes easily with a fork, about 10 minutes.

In a small saucepan over high heat, heat the vegetable oil. Add the garlic. When it sizzles, the oil is ready. Pour the hot oil over the fish and sprinkle with soy sauce. Garnish with the green onions.

NOTE: This recipe can also be cooked in the microwave. Place fish fillets on a plate, cover loosely with plastic wrap, and microwave on high for 2 minutes. Let stand for 2 minutes. Rotate the plate and microwave for an additional 3 minutes.

steamed tofu with sun-dried scallops

Sun-dried scallops can be found at Asian markets. They have a unique and flavorful taste and are considered a delicacy. This dish is well suited for any special occasion. Since you may store the scallops in your pantry, they're perfect to keep on hand for unexpected guests.

3	ounces sun-dried scallops	¼	cup chopped green onions
3	teaspoons vegetable oil, divided	2	tablespoons cornstarch
1	teaspoon minced garlic	1	teaspoon sesame oil
4	ounces shrimp, peeled and deveined	½	teaspoon salt
12	ounces soft tofu	2	tablespoons oyster sauce
1	egg, slightly beaten		

Soak the sun-dried scallops in hot water for 20 minutes, or until soft. Remove the muscles from the sides of the scallops; drain. Rinse in warm water; drain.

In a small saucepan, heat 1 teaspoon vegetable oil. Add the garlic and scallops and stir-fry for 1 minute. Remove to a bowl and let cool.

Rinse the shrimp and pat dry with paper towels. Chop the shrimp. In a medium bowl, mash the tofu with a fork. Stir in the shrimp, egg, green onions, cornstarch, the remaining 2 teaspoons vegetable oil, the sesame oil, salt, and cooked scallops and mix well. Place the mixture in a circle on a heatproof 9-inch pie dish and place the dish on a rack in a steamer. Cover and steam over boiling water for 10 minutes. Turn off the heat and let set for 5 minutes. Cut into 6 wedges, drizzle with the oyster sauce, and serve immediately.

steamed whole fish

When I was growing up, steamed fish was an everyday dish. The preparation is very basic for this recipe; just be sure to use fresh fish and clean and dry it thoroughly. You can change the recipe by using different seasonings, such as black beans or chili peppers, and garnishing with garlic, chopped cilantro, green onions, or shredded peppers. You can also increase the ginger for a stronger flavor. Serve with any stir-fry dish—vegetable, meat, or poultry.

2	tablespoons salted black beans	½	teaspoon salt
1½	pounds whole walleye or red snapper, well cleaned	¼	teaspoon sugar
		1	teaspoon soy sauce
1	teaspoon finely chopped fresh ginger	¼	teaspoon sesame oil
2	tablespoons vegetable oil	2	green onions, with tops
1	teaspoon minced garlic		

In a small bowl, place the black beans and cover with warm water. Stir the beans for about 2 minutes to remove the excess salt. Remove the beans from the water, rinse, and drain well.

Slash the fish crosswise 3 times on each side. In a small bowl, mix the ginger, vegetable oil, black beans, garlic, salt, sugar, soy sauce, and sesame oil; rub the cavity and outside of the fish with the mixture. Cover and refrigerate 30 minutes or longer.

Cut the green onions into 2-inch pieces; shred lengthwise into fine strips. Place in a bowl with ice water to cover; let stand 10 minutes, or until the strips curl. Place the fish on a heatproof plate (see Note). Place the plate on a rack in a steamer, cover, and steam over boiling water until the fish flakes easily with a fork, about 10 minutes. (Add boiling water if necessary.) Garnish with the green onions.

NOTE: If you want to cook this dish in the microwave, cover the fish with plastic wrap on a microwave dish and cook for 3 minutes on high. Let stand for 2 minutes and rotate the dish. Cook an additional 2 minutes on high.

stir-fried seafood
with snow peas

serves 4

This is good to make when you have a small amount of fish, shrimp, or scallops left over from another recipe. It goes well with any type of vegetable and is an attractive dish to prepare for company. Serve with rice.

1¼ teaspoons salt, divided	2 green onions, with tops
6 ounces large shrimp, peeled and deveined	2 tablespoons oyster sauce
6 ounces medium sea scallops	2 tablespoons vegetable oil
4 teaspoons cornstarch, divided	1 teaspoon finely chopped fresh ginger
⅛ teaspoon white pepper	1 teaspoon minced garlic
⅛ teaspoon sesame oil	½ cup canned sliced bamboo shoots
4 ounces snow peas	¼ cup Chicken Broth (page 52)

In a medium bowl, place 2 cups warm water and add 1 teaspoon salt; stir to dissolve. Place the shrimp in the salt water and swirl. Leave the shrimp in the salt water for 5 minutes, then rinse with cold water and drain. Pat dry with paper towels.

Rinse the scallops under cold water 3 or 4 times; drain thoroughly. Pat dry with paper towels.

In a medium bowl, toss the shrimp and scallops with 1 teaspoon cornstarch, ¼ teaspoon salt, the pepper, and sesame oil. Set aside.

Remove the strings from the snow peas. Bring a small pot of water to a boil. Place the snow peas in the boiling water, cover, and cook for 1 minute; drain. Immediately rinse in cold water; drain.

Cut the green onions diagonally into 1-inch pieces.

In a small bowl, mix together the oyster sauce, 2 tablespoons water, and the remaining 1 tablespoon cornstarch. Set aside.

Heat a wok over high heat. Add the vegetable oil and tilt the wok to coat the sides. Add the shrimp, scallops, ginger, and garlic; stir-fry until the scallops are white, about 2 minutes.

Add the bamboo shoots and stir-fry for 1 minute. Add the broth and heat to boiling. Stir in the cornstarch mixture and cook and stir until thickened, about 2 minutes. Add the snow peas and green onions and stir-fry for 30 seconds. Serve immediately.

stuffed eggplant with shrimp and tofu

The combination of shrimp and tofu gives a tender texture to this dish. You can use all shrimp (add 4 ounces to recipe) if you do not want the tofu; the suffing will be thinner without it.

1	pound eggplant	1	egg
1½	teaspoons salt, divided	¼	teaspoon white pepper
12	ounces shrimp, peeled and deveined	4	ounces firm tofu
2	tablespoons hoisin sauce	¼	cup chopped green onions
1	tablespoon chili paste	¼	cup vegetable oil
3	teaspoons sesame oil, divided	2	tablespoons cilantro leaves
2	tablespoons cornstarch		

Wash the eggplant and cut into ½-inch slices (keep the skin on the eggplant). If the eggplant is small, slice it diagonally. Soak in cold water for 10 minutes.

In a medium bowl, place 2 cups warm water and add 1 teaspoon salt; stir to dissolve. Place the shrimp in the salt water and swirl. Leave the shrimp in the salt water for 5 minutes, then rinse with cold water and drain. Pat dry with paper towels.

In a small bowl, mix together the hoisin sauce, chili paste, and 1 teaspoon sesame oil and set aside.

Place the shrimp, cornstarch, egg, the remaining 2 teaspoons sesame oil, the remaining ½ teaspoon salt, and the pepper into a food processor and chop to a paste. Add tofu and combine until smooth. Remove and place in a bowl. Stir in the chopped green onions.

Drain the eggplant slices and pat dry. Place 2 tablespoons filling on top of each eggplant slice and flatten to cover the eggplant. Repeat the process until all the filling is used.

Heat a large nonstick skillet over high heat, and add the vegetable oil. Panfry the stuffed eggplant for 1 minute, then turn over often while cooking and continue frying until both sides are golden brown, about 3 minutes.

Turn the heat down to medium if the slices start to burn. Brush the sauce mixture over the eggplant.

Remove from the pan, place on a heated platter, and garnish with the cilantro leaves.

sweet-and-sour fish

This recipe is quite versatile as you may use shrimp, scallops, or almost any type of fish, frying it in the same batter and topping it with the sweet-and-sour sauce.

1½	pounds walleye or halibut fillets	6	tablespoons cornstarch, divided
1	large egg white	¼	teaspoon baking soda
1	teaspoon salt	4	cups + 2 tablespoons vegetable oil, divided
2	teaspoons finely chopped fresh ginger	1	cup sugar
	Pinch white pepper	1	cup Chicken Broth (page 52)
2	teaspoons sesame oil	¾	cup white vinegar
1	medium carrot, peeled	2	teaspoons dark soy sauce
1	green bell pepper	1	teaspoon minced garlic
¼	cup all-purpose flour	1	(8¼-ounce) can pineapple chunks, drained

Remove and discard the skin from the fish fillets. Cut the fillets into 2 × ½-inch pieces.

In a large bowl, blend the egg white, salt, ginger, white pepper, and sesame oil. Toss the fish with the mixture and set aside.

Cut the carrot diagonally into thin slices. Core and seed the green pepper, cut it into 2 × ½-inch strips, and set aside. In a saucepan, place 1 cup water and the carrot slices and bring to a boil. Cook for 1 minute and drain; set aside.

To prepare the batter, in a medium bowl, place the flour, ¼ cup cornstarch, the baking soda, ¼ cup cold water, and 1 tablespoon vegetable oil and mix well; set aside.

To make the sauce, mix the remaining 2 tablespoons cornstarch with 2 tablespoons water in a small bowl and set aside. In a 2-quart saucepan, place the sugar, chicken broth, vinegar, soy sauce, 1 tablespoon vegetable oil, and the garlic. Bring to a boil and stir in the cornstarch mixture. Cook until the sauce is thickened, 1 to 2 minutes. Remove from the heat and set aside.

In a wok or large, deep skillet, heat the remaining 4 cups vegetable oil to 350°F. Combine the fish fillets with the batter. Deep-fry half the fish pieces until light brown, 2 to 3 minutes, stirring to separate them. Drain on paper towels. Increase the oil temperature to 375°F. and refry the fish pieces for 1 minute. Drain again. Place on a large serving platter. Reheat the sauce and add the carrot, green pepper, and pineapple chunks and bring to a boil. Turn off the heat, pour over the fish, and serve.

tea-smoked sea bass

This is a wonderful recipe that shows you how to create an authentic smoky Asian flavor in your conventional oven. You may also use red snapper.

1½	pounds skinless sea bass fillets		1	tablespoon white vinegar
1½	teaspoons salt, divided		2	teaspoons sugar
1	teaspoon finely chopped fresh ginger		2	teaspoons sesame oil
1	tablespoon vegetable oil		2	tablespoons tea leaves
⅛	teaspoon white pepper		1	cup (light or dark) brown sugar
2	teaspoons soy sauce		¼	cup uncooked rice
1	English (seedless) cucumber			

Cut the sea bass into 4 to 5 pieces and wipe dry with paper towels.

To prepare the marinade, in a small bowl, combine 1 teaspoon salt, the ginger, vegetable oil, pepper, and soy sauce. Rub the marinade on all sides of the fish and marinate for 30 minutes or longer in the refrigerator.

Preheat the oven to 500°F.

Slice the cucumber very thinly. In a medium bowl, blend the vinegar, sugar, sesame oil, and remaining ½ teaspoon salt. Add the cucumber and toss. Let soak for 10 minutes. Discard the excess dressing and place the cucumber slices in an overlapping pattern around the edge of a serving platter.

Line the inside surface of a large covered Dutch oven or wok completely with heavy foil. In the foil-lined pan (see Note), mix together the tea leaves, brown sugar, and rice. Spread out evenly. Place a metal steam rack on the tea leaves, which stands at least 1 inch above. Place the marinated fish on the rack. Cover the pan tightly. (The tea leaves and brown sugar will smoke the fish, so be sure the pan is tightly covered. If the cover doesn't fit tight enough, place foil around the outside of the cover and pan.) Place in the preheated oven for 15 minutes. Remove from the oven and let sit, covered, for 5 minutes. Carefully open the lid. Using a spatula, carefully transfer the fish to the platter.

NOTE: If you use too heavy a pan, you will not get enough heat in the oven to brown the sugar and produce the smoky flavor.

tofu crabmeat
medallions

Serve these Asian crabcakes over a salad or stir-fried vegetables for a light and healthy meal. It goes well with fried rice. If using Yeung Chau Fried Rice (page 177), omit the shrimp and chicken.

14	ounces firm tofu	6	ounces crabmeat, drained and picked over
1	small egg white	1	teaspoon sesame oil
½	teaspoon salt	4	tablespoons mayonnaise
¼	teaspoon white pepper	1	tablespoon hot red pepper sauce
1	tablespoon cornstarch		About 4 cups vegetable oil

Preheat the oven to 375°F.

Using a fork, in a medium bowl, mash the tofu and add the egg white, salt, white pepper, and cornstarch. Mix well.

In a small bowl, mix together the crabmeat and the sesame oil. Add the tofu mixture and mix well.

In a small bowl, mix the mayonnaise with the red pepper sauce for a dip.

Form the tofu mixture into ¼-cup patties and place on a cookie sheet (the patties should be ½ inch thick). Cook in the oven for 10 minutes.

In a wok or large, deep skillet, heat about 2 inches of vegetable oil to 350°F. Deep-fry the tofu patties to golden brown, about 3 minutes. Remove and drain on paper towels. Serve with the red pepper sauce dip.

walnut shrimp

This is a popular dish made in Hong Kong, where chefs often use mayonnaise in banquet dishes. You may omit the walnuts if you prefer.

1	teaspoon salt	4	cups + 1 teaspoon vegetable oil, divided
1	pound extra-large shrimp, peeled and deveined	½	cup sweetened condensed milk
1	large egg white	¼	cup mayonnaise
¼	cup cornstarch	2	teaspoons lemon juice
⅛	teaspoon baking soda	2	teaspoons lime juice
⅛	teaspoon garlic salt	½	cup Candied Walnuts (page 180)

Place 2 cups warm water in a bowl and add the salt; stir to dissolve. Place the shrimp in the salt water and swirl. Leave the shrimp in the salt water for 5 minutes, then rinse with cold water and drain. Pat dry with paper towels.

In a small bowl, mix together the egg white, cornstarch, baking soda, garlic salt, and 1 teaspoon vegetable oil to a smooth paste. Add the shrimp and blend to coat very well.

In another small bowl, mix together the sweetened condensed milk, mayonnaise, and lemon and lime juices until smooth. Set aside.

In a wok or large, deep nonstick skillet, heat the remaining 4 cups oil to 350°F. Deep-fry the shrimp until light brown, 3 to 4 minutes, turning as necessary. Remove from the oil. Increase the oil temperature to 375°F. Cook the shrimp for 1 more minute and remove; drain well on paper towels.

Pour the mayonnaise mixture over the shrimp and stir until well covered.

Place on a platter, sprinkle the candied walnuts over, and serve.

vegetables

Asparagus with Wild Mushrooms

Braised Stuffed Tofu

Butternut Squash with Salted Black Beans

Celestial Tofu

Chinese Long Beans with Black Mushrooms

Green Beans with Cashews

Harvest Delight

Hot-and-Sour Cabbage

Hot-and-Sour Stir-Fried Celery

Jewel of Happiness

Stir-Fried Asian Eggplant

Stir-Fried Green Beans with Tomato and Tofu

Zen Palate

Zucchini with Salted Black Beans

asparagus with
wild mushrooms

serves 4

Mushrooms work well with just about any type of vegetable. This goes very well with one of the fish recipes.

4	ounces fresh shiitake or oyster mushrooms (see Note)	2	teaspoons minced garlic
1	pound asparagus	½	teaspoon salt
2	teaspoons cornstarch	1	tablespoon oyster sauce
1	tablespoon vegetable oil	½	cup Chicken Broth (page 52)

Rinse the mushrooms in cold water; drain. Remove and discard the stems. Cut the caps into 1-inch strips. Wash the asparagus thoroughly. Break off the tough ends of the asparagus as far down as the stalk snaps easily. In a small bowl, mix together the cornstarch and 2 teaspoons cold water.

Heat a wok over high heat. Add the vegetable oil and rotate the wok to coat the sides. Add the garlic, asparagus, and salt and stir-fry for 1 minute. Add the mushrooms and continue to stir-fry until mixed. Stir in the oyster sauce. Stir in the chicken broth and heat to boiling. Stir in the cornstarch mixture; cook and stir until thickened, about 30 seconds. Turn off the heat and remove the asparagus with tongs. Arrange the asparagus across a platter and top with the mushrooms.

NOTE: This recipe would be great with any variety of mushrooms. You may also increase the amount. If the mushrooms are very large, be sure to cut them into smaller pieces.

braised stuffed tofu

This is a great vegetarian dish as it's high in protein and very nutritious. Serve with steamed white rice and stir-fried vegetables for a complete meal.

1	ounce canned Sichuan cabbage (also called preserved vegetable)	14	ounces firm tofu
1	ounce shiitake mushrooms	2	tablespoons vegetable oil, divided
½	teaspoon cornstarch	1	teaspoon finely chopped fresh ginger, divided
	Dash sugar	1	teaspoon finely minced garlic, divided
12	ounces baby bok choy (about 4)	½	teaspoon salt
		3	tablespoons oyster sauce

Rinse the Sichuan cabbage very well and pat dry with paper towels. Chop into very small minced pieces.

Cut off and discard the stems from the mushrooms. Wash the mushrooms with cold water. Pat dry with paper towels and mince very fine. In a small bowl, mix the mushrooms with the Sichuan cabbage. Sprinkle with the cornstarch and sugar and set aside.

Rinse the bok choy with cold water and pat dry with paper towels. Cut each baby bok choy crosswise 4 times. Cut the tofu into 12 squares, about 1½ inches square by ¾ inch thick. Set the tofu squares on a cloth to drain the excess water out. Scoop some tofu out of the center of each square, reserving the scooped-out tofu. With a fork, mash about half of the scooped-out tofu and add to the mushroom mixture (it should be the consistency of paste). Put about 1 teaspoon of the mixture in each square of tofu, being very careful not to tear the tofu. Pat the filling down carefully. Repeat until all 12 pieces are filled and set aside.

Heat a large nonstick pan or wok over high heat. Add 1 tablespoon vegetable oil and stir-fry the baby bok choy for 1 minute. Add ½ teaspoon ginger, ½ teaspoon garlic, and the salt, and stir well. Add 2 tablespoons water and cook until the vegetables change color, about 2 minutes. Remove the bok choy to a platter.

Wash the pan and reheat with the remaining 1 tablespoon vegetable oil, ½ teaspoon ginger, and ½ teaspoon garlic. Carefully place the stuffed tofu squares, one at a time, in the pan and panfry both sides until slightly brown, about 2 minutes. Add more oil if needed.

Add the oyster sauce and coat the squares. Cook until the sauce is absorbed into the tofu, about 2 minutes. Turn off the heat and place the tofu on top of the baby bok choy. Serve immediately.

butternut squash with salted black beans

Salted black beans are actually fermented and marinated soybeans. You may substitute packaged Japanese miso as an alternative. To get all of the skin off the squash, you will have to use a knife: a vegetable peeler won't get enough of the peel off.

1	medium butternut squash (about 2 pounds)	½	cup Chicken Broth (page 52) or Vegetable Broth (page 54)
3	tablespoons salted black beans		
1	teaspoon cornstarch	2	teaspoons soy sauce
1	tablespoon vegetable oil	1	cup green onions, with tops, cut into 1-inch pieces
1	teaspoon minced garlic		

Cut the squash in half and discard the seeds. Remove the skin, cut the squash again lengthwise, and cut the squash crosswise into ¼-inch slices.

Place the black beans in a small bowl. Cover with warm water, soak for 5 minutes, and then drain. Rinse 3 to 4 times to remove the excess salt and loose skins and drain well.

In a small bowl, mix together the cornstarch and 1 teaspoon water.

Heat a wok or nonstick skillet over high heat. Add the vegetable oil, black beans, garlic, and squash. Stir-fry over high heat for 2 minutes and add the broth. Cover and cook for 3 minutes. Add the soy sauce and stir well. Stir in the cornstarch mixture and cook until the sauce thickens, 1 to 2 minutes. Add the green onions, stir, and cook for 30 more seconds.

celestial tofu

Tofu is a good substitute for meat. It is loaded with protein, and when served with vegetables makes a complete meal. The sauce is spicy, so it's a good idea to serve it with rice.

14	ounces firm tofu		**sauce**
1	green bell pepper	1	tablespoon brown bean sauce
2	Thai hot red chili peppers, rinsed	1	teaspoon minced garlic
		1	teaspoon sugar
		1	teaspoon sesame oil
		1	tablespoon vegetable oil

Cut the tofu into ¾-inch diced pieces. Seed and core the green pepper and cut it into ½-inch squares. Seed the chili peppers and cut them into ½-inch squares.

To make the sauce, in a small bowl, mix together the brown bean sauce, garlic, sugar, and sesame oil.

Heat a wok or large skillet over high heat. Add the vegetable oil and tilt to coat the sides of the pan. Add the sauce mixture and heat for 10 seconds. Add the tofu and green peppers and stir-fry for 2 minutes. Add the red chili peppers and continue to stir until all the ingredients are well mixed, about 1 minute. Serve hot.

chinese long beans with black mushrooms

Chinese long beans can be found at Asian markets and some grocery stores. The beans should be firm and should be used right away. You may substitute green beans.

8	ounces long green beans		¼	cup Vegetable Broth (page 54) or Chicken Broth (page 52)
½	ounce dried black mushrooms			Pinch salt
1	small red pepper		2	tablespoons chili paste (see Note)
2	tablespoons vegetable oil, divided		1	teaspoon sugar
1	cup sliced onion			
2	teaspoons minced garlic			

Rinse the long green beans in cold water and cut into 2-inch pieces.

Soak the mushrooms in hot water for 20 minutes, or until soft; drain. Rinse in warm water and drain. Squeeze out the excess moisture. Remove and discard the stems; cut the caps into ¼-inch-thin strips.

Core and seed the red pepper and cut into ½-inch strips. Set aside.

Heat a wok or large skillet over medium heat. Add 1 tablespoon vegetable oil, the sliced onion, and garlic and stir-fry for 30 seconds. Add the green beans and black mushrooms and stir-fry for 1 minute, then add the vegetable or chicken broth and salt. Stir well, cover, and cook for 1 minute. Uncover, turn the heat up to high, and continue stir-frying until all the liquid is absorbed, about 1 minute. Add the remaining 1 tablespoon vegetable oil, the chili paste, sugar, and red pepper strips and stir-fry for 1 minute.

NOTE: This dish is very spicy. If you want a milder version, substitute oyster sauce for the chili paste.

green beans with cashews

Green beans with slivered almonds is a nice variation. This goes well with any of the fish recipes and rice.

1	pound green beans	2	tablespoons hoisin sauce
2	tablespoons vegetable oil	2	tablespoons oyster sauce
2	teaspoons minced garlic	2	ounces roasted cashews

Rinse the green beans with cold water and drain. Snap off both ends. Break the beans in half or in 2-inch pieces.

Heat a wok or skillet over high heat. Add the vegetable oil and green beans and stir-fry for 2 minutes. Add the garlic, hoisin sauce, and oyster sauce and continue to stir-fry for 30 seconds.

Remove to a serving platter and garnish with the roasted cashews. Serve immediately.

harvest delight

Use any fresh vegetables from your garden or what is in season at the market.

8	ounces bok choy	2	tablespoons vegetable oil, divided
1	red bell pepper	1	teaspoon salt, divided
4	ounces snow peas	1	teaspoon minced garlic

Wash the bok choy with cold water, drain, and remove the leaves from the bok choy stems. Reserve the leaves for another use, such as soup. Cut the stems diagonally into ¼-inch slices.

Core and seed the red pepper and cut it into 2 × ¼-inch strips.

Remove and discard the strings from the snow peas. Rinse the peas with cold water and drain. Set aside.

Heat a wok or a large nonstick skillet over high heat. Add 1 tablespoon vegetable oil, the bok choy, ½ teaspoon salt, and the garlic and stir-fry for 3 minutes. Remove and place the bok choy in the center of a serving platter in a long row, with the slices overlapping.

Reheat the wok, add 2 teaspoons vegetable oil, the red pepper, and the remaining ½ teaspoon salt, and stir-fry for 2 minutes. Remove from the wok and place the peppers at the top of the serving platter, above the bok choy.

Add 2 cups water to the wok and bring to a boil. Add the snow peas and cook over high heat until the water returns to boiling. Add the remaining 1 teaspoon vegetable oil and cook 30 seconds. Drain and place the snow peas at the bottom of the serving platter. Serve immediately.

hot-and-sour cabbage

Cabbage is excellent for everyday cooking, and it keeps longer in the refrigerator than most other vegetables. If you prefer a less spicy dish, use less chili pepper or omit completely. This recipe goes well with grilled burgers, pork chops, or any barbecued meat. It can also be served cold.

1	small cabbage	2	tablespoons vegetable oil
2	green onions	1	tablespoon minced garlic
½	cup ketchup	3	Thai red hot chili peppers, seeded and thinly sliced
1	tablespoon sugar		
2	teaspoons soy sauce	½	teaspoon salt
2	teaspoons cornstarch		

Remove the core from the cabbage, then cut the cabbage into 1½ × 1-inch pieces. Cut the green onions into 1-inch pieces, including the tops.

In a small bowl, combine the ketchup, sugar, and soy sauce. Set aside.

In a small bowl, mix the cornstarch with 1 tablespoon water. Set aside.

Heat a wok or skillet over high heat. Add the vegetable oil, garlic, cabbage, and Thai chili peppers and stir-fry for 1 minute. Add the salt and sauce mixture and continue to stir-fry over high heat until the cabbage is tender, about 3 minutes. Stir in the cornstarch mixture; cook and stir until thickened, about 30 seconds. Add the green onions and stir-fry for 1 minute. Remove to a heated platter and serve.

hot-and-sour
stir-fried celery

You can use less celery and add some red or green bell peppers. If you want a spicier dish, add more chili peppers.

8	celery stalks	2	teaspoons sugar
1	tablespoon vegetable oil	1	teaspoon light soy sauce
2	teaspoons minced garlic	2	teaspoons sesame oil
½	teaspoon salt	1	hot red chili pepper, seeded and thinly sliced
4	teaspoons white vinegar		

Remove and discard the leaves of the celery and the stringy stalks. Cut the stalks into 2 × ¼-inch slices.

Heat a wok or skillet over high heat. Add the vegetable oil, garlic, celery, and salt and stir-fry for 1 minute. Turn the heat down to medium and stir-fry an additional 2 minutes. Add the vinegar, sugar, soy sauce, sesame oil, and chili pepper and stir-fry over high heat for 1 more minute. Remove and serve hot or cold.

jewel of happiness

Lotus root symbolizes happiness and fertility. It's a starchy and dense root that is quite filling. Pair it with Tea-Smoked Sea Bass (page 143) for a light and healthy dinner.

1	pound fresh lotus root (see Note)	2	tablespoons sugar
2	Thai hot red chili peppers, seeded and thinly sliced	1	tablespoon light soy sauce
		1	tablespoon sesame oil
2	tablespoons white vinegar		

Wash the fresh lotus root in cold water. Trim off and discard both ends of the lotus root and peel off the skin. Cut the root into ⅛-inch-thin slices. In a saucepan of boiling water, place the root, return to boiling, and cook for 1 minute. Drain and place in a medium bowl. Add the chili peppers.

In a small saucepan, place the vinegar, 1 tablespoon water, the sugar, soy sauce, and sesame oil and bring to a boil. Stir until the sugar is dissolved. Pour over the blanched lotus root and the chili peppers and chill for 1 hour.

NOTE: Fresh lotus root is only available in the springtime.

stir-fried asian eggplant

You will find Asian eggplant at many Asian markets. You can substitute regular eggplant, just cut it lengthwise into 4 to 6 strips before slicing.

4	Asian eggplants		1	teaspoon sesame oil
2	teaspoons salt		2	tablespoons vegetable oil
1	tablespoon oyster sauce		2	teaspoons minced garlic
1	teaspoon sugar		2	hot red chili peppers, seeded and thinly sliced

Cut each eggplant in half lengthwise, then cut diagonally into ½-inch slices. Cover the eggplants with water, add the salt, and stir to dissolve the salt. Soak the eggplants for 5 minutes, then drain well.

In a small bowl, mix the oyster sauce with the sugar and sesame oil and set aside.

Heat a wok or nonstick skillet over high heat. Add the vegetable oil, garlic, chili peppers, and eggplants and stir-fry for 2 minutes. Add 2 tablespoons water and continue stir-frying for 2 more minutes. Add the oyster sauce mixture and stir well to mix. Remove to a platter and serve hot or cold.

stir-fried green beans with tomato and tofu

serves 4

Tofu is very high in protein and a great alternative to meat, whether you're a vegetarian or not. This is a fast, easy, colorful, and healthy dish. Serve this with rice.

3   tablespoons vegetable oil, divided
10 ounces tofu, cut into 1 × 1 × ½-inch slices
1   tablespoon oyster sauce
1   cup sliced onion
1   teaspoon minced garlic

8   ounces green beans
¼   cup Chicken Broth (page 52) or Vegetable Broth (page 54)
2   tomatoes
1   tablespoon chili paste

Heat a wok or large nonstick skillet over high heat (it is easier to cook tofu in a nonstick pan). Add 2 tablespoons vegetable oil and the tofu. Carefully turn over a few times and panfry until lightly brown, about 2 minutes per side. Add the oyster sauce and gently simmer, about 2 minutes, making sure the tofu doesn't break into pieces. Remove the tofu and place on a platter.

Reheat the wok or skillet, add the remaining 1 tablespoon vegetable oil, the onion, garlic, and green beans, and stir fry for 1 minute. Add the chicken or vegetable broth and cover. Cook for 1 minute. Uncover and continue to stir-fry until all the liquid is absorbed, about 2 minutes. Add the tomatoes and chili paste and stir until well mixed, about 1 minute. Place the tofu back in the pan and gently mix together.

zen palate

Experiment with a variety of vegetables for this dish. Keep canned baby corn, straw mushrooms, and water chestnuts in your pantry as staples for this and other Asian dishes. Pair this festive recipe with Butternut Squash with Salted Black Beans (page 149) for a complete vegan meal.

2 ounces cellophane noodles (bean thread)	½ cup gingko nuts (fresh or canned; see Note)
½ ounce dried tiger lily buds	½ teaspoon salt
1 ounce dried black mushrooms	½ cup Vegetable Broth (page 54) or water
3 large stalks celery cabbage (Napa cabbage)	2 tablespoons light soy sauce
4 ounces snow peas	2 green onions, with tops, cut into 1-inch pieces
4 ounces jicama	1 teaspoon sesame oil
2 tablespoons vegetable oil	
1 teaspoon minced garlic	

Soak the cellophane noodles in warm water for 5 minutes; drain and set aside. Soak the tiger lily buds in warm water for 5 minutes, rinse with cold water, and remove and discard the tips. Soak the black mushrooms in hot water for 15 minutes, or until soft. Rinse with cold water and drain; remove and discard the stems. Cut the caps into ½-inch pieces. Rinse the celery cabbage in cold water and drain. Cut the stalks crosswise into ½-inch pieces. Remove and discard the strings from the snow pea pods. In a saucepan of boiling water, place the snow peas and return the water to a boil. Drain, immediately rinse in cold water, drain again, and set aside. Peel the jicama and cut into 2 × ¼-inch strips.

Heat a wok or large skillet over high heat. Add the vegetable oil, garlic, tiger lily buds, black mushrooms, celery cabbage, gingko nuts, and jicama and stir-fry for 2 minutes. Add the salt, vegetable broth, soy sauce, and cellophane noodles and cook for 1 minute. Add the snow peas, green onions, and sesame oil and stir-fry for 1 more minute. Serve immediately.

NOTE: If you buy fresh gingko nuts, the hard shell will need to be removed. Pound with a hammer to remove the skins. These nuts can be bought at Asian stores.

zucchini with
salted black beans

Smaller-size zucchini are ideal for stir-frying. Make sure to wash the zucchini thoroughly to remove dirt and sand.

1	pound yellow zucchini		1	teaspoon minced garlic
3	tablespoons salted black beans		1	teaspoon sugar
1	small white onion		2	green onions, with tops, cut into 1-inch pieces
2	tablespoons vegetable oil		1	tablespoon oyster sauce

Wash and dry the zucchini. Remove the ends and cut in half lengthwise and then cut into ¼-inch slices.

In a small bowl, place the salted black beans, cover with warm water, and soak for 5 minutes. Drain and rinse 3 to 4 times to remove the excess salt and loose skins. Drain well.

Cut the onion in half. Cut each half into ¼-inch slices, to yield about 1¼ cups.

Heat a nonstick skillet over high heat. Add the vegetable oil, onion, and garlic and stir-fry for 30 seconds. Add the salted black beans and sugar. Add the zucchini and stir-fry 2 to 3 minutes. Add the green onions and oyster sauce and stir-fry for 30 seconds. Serve.

mussels with cilantro sauce
(page 130)

walnut shrimp *(page 145)*

braised stuffed tofu *(page 148)*

butternut squash with salted black beans *(page 149)*

top to bottom: stir-fried asian eggplant *(page 157)*
and salmon with tofu *(page 135)*

asparagus with wild mushrooms *(page 147)*

stir-fried pork and broccoli
with egg noodles (*page 175*)

pineapple fried rice (*page 169*)

raspberry almond float (*page 179*)

mango pudding *(page 182)*

noodles and rice

Beef Chow Fun

Homemade Egg Noodles

Black Mushrooms and Broccoli with Egg Noodles

Canton-Style Chicken Chow Mein

Egg Noodles with Pork and Sichuan Sauce

Jasmine Rice

Noodles with Peanut Sauce

Pineapple Fried Rice

Rice Bowl with Mussels and Asparagus

Rice Noodle Salad with Ham

Roast Beef and Rice Noodles

Shrimp with Garlic Noodles

Soy-Flavored Rice Noodles with Beef

Stir-Fried Pork and Broccoli with Egg Noodles

Stir-Fried Shrimp with Spaghetti Noodles

Yeung Chau Fried Rice

beef chow fun

"Fun" means wide rice noodle. You can find them fresh or dried at Asian markets. It isn't necessary to boil fresh noodles; they can simply be added to the beef when stir-frying. This is a hearty dish that can be served as a complete meal.

6	ounces dried wide rice noodles or 10 ounces fresh wide rice noodles		Dash white pepper
1	teaspoon sesame oil	8	ounces asparagus
½	ounce medium dried black mushrooms (see Note)	2	ounces snow peas
		2	green onions, with tops
8	ounces beef flank or boneless sirloin steak	¾	cup Chicken Broth (page 52), divided
2	tablespoons + 1 teaspoon cornstarch, divided	2	tablespoons oyster sauce
1¼	teaspoons salt, divided	3	tablespoons vegetable oil
2	teaspoons sugar, divided	1	teaspoon finely chopped fresh ginger
		1	teaspoon minced garlic

Soak the dried rice noodles in warm water for 15 minutes; drain. Rinse with cold water. In a large saucepan, bring 6 cups water to a boil. Add the rice noodles and cook for 30 seconds, stirring to separate. Drain the noodles and mix with the sesame oil. Divide the noodles evenly into 2 or 3 bowls and set aside.

Soak the mushrooms in hot water until soft, about 20 minutes; drain. Remove and discard the stems; cut the caps into ½-inch pieces.

Trim the fat from the beef. Cut the beef with the grain into 2-inch strips. Cut strips across the grain into 1 × ¼-inch slices. In a bowl, toss the beef, 1 teaspoon cornstarch, 1 teaspoon salt, 1 teaspoon sugar, and the pepper. Cover and refrigerate for 20 minutes.

Break off and discard the tough ends of the asparagus as far down as the stalks snap easily. Cut the asparagus into 2-inch pieces. Remove and discard the strings from the snow peas. In a saucepan of boiling water, place the peas, cover, and cook for 1 minute. Drain, immediately rinse under cold running water, and drain again. Cut the green onions into 2-inch pieces, cut the pieces lengthwise into thin strips, and set aside.

In a small bowl, mix ¼ cup chicken broth, the remaining 2 tablespoons cornstarch, the remaining ¼ teaspoon salt, the oyster sauce and the remaining 1 teaspoon sugar and set aside.

Heat a wok or nonstick skillet over high heat. Add 2 tablespoons vegetable oil and tilt to coat the sides of the wok. Add the beef, chopped ginger, and garlic and stir-fry for 3 minutes, or until the beef is brown. Remove the beef from the wok. Wash and thoroughly dry the wok.

Reheat the wok over high heat and add the remaining 1 tablespoon vegetable oil. Add the mushrooms and asparagus and stir and cook for 2 minutes. Add the remaining ½ cup chicken broth and the cornstarch mixture and cook until thickened, about 2 minutes. Add the snow peas and cook for 30 seconds. Add the beef; cook and stir until the beef is hot. Pour the beef mixture evenly over each bowl of noodles, garnish with the chopped onions, and serve.

NOTE: A cup of sliced fresh mushrooms can be substituted for the cut-up rehydrated black mushrooms.

homemade egg noodles

serves 2 to 3

You can freeze homemade noodles for up to 3 months or keep them for up to 2 days in the refrigerator. Making noodles is a fun rainy day project for the whole family. Egg noodles are extremely versatile and can be used in a variety of soups and stir-fries.

1¼ cups all-purpose or semolina flour	2 large eggs (about ½ cup; add water if you have less)

In a medium bowl, mix together the flour and eggs to make a dough. Knead the dough on a lightly floured surface until elastic. Form into a ball and let rest for 15 minutes.

Using a rolling pin to roll the dough into an oval sheet, roll the dough outward until very thin. On a lightly floured cloth, place the dough so that one third of it is on the cloth and two thirds of the sheet hangs off the table or counter. Carefully stretch the sheet out further.

Lightly flour the sheet and roll it up into about a 3-inch-diameter tube. Flatten and use a sharp knife to slice the dough into very thin noodles. Separate the noodles and form them into a nest.

You may now use the noodles in any noodle recipe. You can boil them in chicken stock to make soup. You can panfry them in oil and garlic and top with soy sauce. You can top them with any stir-fry combination.

black mushrooms and broccoli with egg noodles

You can change this meatless recipe by adding leftover chicken, barbecued pork, or seafood. Just cut the meat into small pieces and add before you add the broth, to make a complete meal in one dish.

6	medium dried black mushrooms	8	ounces dried egg noodles or 14 ounces fresh
¼	teaspoon salt		egg noodles (page 163)
	Pinch white pepper	2	tablespoons vegetable oil
2	tablespoons + ½ teaspoon cornstarch, divided	2	teaspoons minced garlic
		2	tablespoons white wine
10	ounces broccoli	1	cup Chicken Broth (page 52)
2	tablespoons oyster sauce	1	green onion, shredded

Soak the dried mushrooms in hot water for 20 minutes, or until soft. Discard the stems and cut the mushroom caps into thin strips. In a medium bowl, combine the mushrooms with the salt, pepper, and ½ teaspoon cornstarch.

Remove the florets from the broccoli, keeping 1 inch of the stem. Cut the rest of the stems diagonally into ¼-inch slices, discarding the last inch of stem. Place the broccoli in a saucepan of boiling water and return to a boil. Cook for 1 minute and drain. Immediately rinse in cold water, drain well, and set aside.

In a small bowl, mix together the remaining 2 tablespoons cornstarch, the oyster sauce, and 2 tablespoons water.

Bring a large pot of water to a boil over high heat. Add the noodles and cook until almost al dente, about 5 minutes for dried noodles, 3 for fresh noodles. Drain well and set aside.

Heat a large nonstick skillet over high heat. Add the vegetable oil, garlic, and noodles and panfry until the underside is browned, about 3 minutes. Flip over and brown the other side, 2 to 3 minutes more. Remove to a platter. Add the mushrooms and stir-fry for 1 minute. Add the white wine and stir well. Add the broccoli and chicken broth and bring to a boil. Stir in the cornstarch mixture and cook, stirring constantly, until thickened, about 1 minute. Pour the mushrooms and sauce over the noodles. Garnish with the shredded green onion and serve immediately.

canton-style chicken chow mein

This recipe is an excellent everyday dish for lunch or dinner. You can use any kind of noodles. You may want to serve with a small dish of soy sauce on the side.

8	ounces skinless, boneless chicken breast	2	tablespoons oyster sauce
¼	teaspoon salt	¼	teaspoon sugar
⅛	teaspoon white pepper	6	ounces dried egg noodles or 10 ounces fresh
1	teaspoon finely chopped fresh ginger		egg noodles (page 163)
2	tablespoons + 1 teaspoon cornstarch, divided	4	tablespoons vegetable oil, divided
4	ounces snow peas	1	teaspoon minced garlic
2	ounces shiitake mushrooms	1	cup Chicken Broth (page 52)
6	ounces bean sprouts		

Cut the chicken breast into ¼-inch strips. In a medium bowl, mix together the salt, pepper, chopped ginger, and 1 teaspoon cornstarch. Add the chicken and toss to blend.

Remove and discard the strings from the snow peas. In a medium pot, bring water to a boil. Add the snow peas and bring the water back to a boil. Drain immediately, rinse in cold water, and drain again.

Rinse the mushrooms with cold water. Remove and discard the stems. Cut the mushroom caps into ½-inch strips.

Rinse the bean sprouts with cold water and drain.

In a small bowl, mix together the oyster sauce, the remaining 2 tablespoons cornstarch, and the sugar. In a large pot, heat water to boiling and stir in the noodles. Return to a boil and cook 5 minutes for dried noodles, 3 minutes for fresh noodles, or until almost al dente. Drain and rinse in cold water. Drain well.

Heat a nonstick skillet over high heat and add 2 tablespoons vegetable oil. Add the noodles and separate to cover the bottom of the skillet, forming a large pancake. Brown, about 3 minutes, and turn over. Brown the other side for 3 minutes. Remove from the pan and add the remaining 2 tablespoons vegetable oil, the chicken, and garlic. Stir-fry for 1 minute and add the mushrooms and bean sprouts. Continue to stir-fry for 2 minutes and add the chicken broth. Cook until boiling and stir in the cornstarch mixture. Cook and stir until thickened, about 2 minutes. Add the snow peas and stir to mix. Serve.

egg noodles with
pork and sichuan sauce

This is a great recipe for lunch or brunch gatherings. It can be doubled and prepared ahead. Keep the sauce and the noodles in separate containers and reheat in the microwave for 2 minutes, covered. Add the sauce to the noodles and garnish with green onions before serving.

8	ounces ground pork	1	teaspoon minced garlic
1¼	teaspoons salt, divided	1	teaspoon cayenne
⅛	teaspoon white pepper	2	tablespoons ground bean paste (page 18)
2	tablespoons + 1 teaspoon cornstarch, divided	¼	teaspoon sugar
1	tablespoon light soy sauce	1	cup canned straw mushrooms
8	ounces fresh egg noodles (page 163)	1¼	cups Chicken Broth (page 52)
1	tablespoon + 2 teaspoons vegetable oil, divided	2	tablespoons chopped green onion

In a medium bowl, mix the ground pork with ¼ teaspoon salt, the pepper, and 1 teaspoon cornstarch. In a small bowl, mix the remaining 2 tablespoons cornstarch, soy sauce, and 2 tablespoons cold water and set aside.

In a Dutch oven, bring 8 cups water to a boil. Add the noodles, the remaining 1 teaspoon salt, and 2 teaspoons vegetable oil. Stir to separate the noodles and return to boiling. Reduce the heat to medium and cook, uncovered, for 3 to 4 minutes, or until the noodles are done, or follow the instructions on the package; drain. Place in a large serving bowl and cover to keep hot.

Heat a wok or large nonstick skillet over high heat. Add the remaining 1 tablespoon vegetable oil and the garlic. Add the ground pork, cayenne, ground bean sauce, and sugar and continue to stir-fry for 2 minutes. Add the mushrooms and chicken broth. Bring to a boil and stir in the cornstarch mixture. Cook until thickened, about 2 minutes. Pour over the egg noodles and garnish with the chopped green onion. Serve immediately.

jasmine rice

There are many kinds of white rice to choose from, but most use the same cooking method. Some long-grain rice is drier and should be rinsed with cold water so it absorbs some moisture before cooking. All rice can be reheated in a microwave, covered with plastic wrap. Leftover rice can also be frozen for up to 3 months. Electric rice cookers are wonderful for cooking rice perfectly every time.

2   cups jasmine rice

Fill a 2-quart saucepan three quarters full of cold water. Add the jasmine rice and swirl around to loosen the starch. Pour out the water slowly and repeat this procedure again. Most of the water should be removed.

Add 2 cups cold water to the rice and cook to a boil over high heat. Stir and cover; reduce the heat to low and simmer for 15 minutes. Do not uncover or the rice will not fully cook. Remove from the heat when cooked. (If not ready to serve, keep warm in a steamer, or the rice may be reheated in a microwave.)

noodles with peanut sauce

Served cold, this is a great luncheon dish or perfect for a lazy Saturday afternoon picnic. If you would like to serve this dish warm, reheat the noodles briefly in boiling water before tossing with the vegetables and peanut sauce. This is a great dish to present to guests and toss with sauce at the table.

6	ounces fresh or dried egg noodles (page 163)		**peanut sauce**
1	teaspoon salt	¼	cup creamy peanut butter
2	teaspoons vegetable oil	2	tablespoons sesame oil
2	green onions, with tops, shredded	3	tablespoons soy sauce
1	small carrot	2½	tablespoons vinegar
1	medium cucumber	2	tablespoons sugar
2	ounces snow peas	3	tablespoons water
		1	tablespoon dry mustard

In a Dutch oven, bring 8 cups water to a boil. Add the noodles, salt, and vegetable oil. Stir to separate the noodles and return to a boil. Reduce the heat to medium and cook, uncovered, for 2 to 3 minutes, or until the noodles are done. Rinse with cold water, drain, and set aside.

Place the green onions in ice water for 10 minutes. Drain well.

Peel the carrot and cut into matchstick strips. Peel the cucumber and slice into 2-inch pieces; then cut into matchstick strips.

Remove and discard the strings from the pea pods. Place the peas in boiling water and return to a boil. Immediately rinse with cold water and drain thoroughly. Cut into ⅛-inch match-stick strips.

To prepare the sauce, in a medium bowl, thoroughly mix the peanut butter, sesame oil, soy sauce, vinegar, sugar, and water.

In a separate bowl, mix the dry mustard with 1 tablespoon water, stirring in one direction until smooth. Add this mixture to the peanut sauce and stir until well mixed.

Place the noodles on a serving platter. Arrange the carrot, cucumber, and snow pea pods in a spoke on top of the noodles. Place the green onions in the center of the spoke. Before serving, pour the peanut sauce over and toss gently.

pineapple fried rice

Served in a pineapple, this recipe makes for an excellent presentation. Fried rice is a wonderful way to use leftover steamed white rice as well as any leftover meat as long as it's cut into small pieces. Light soy sauce enhances the flavor and color of the vegetables and other ingredients. You may cook the rice ahead and simply reheat and place in pineapple shells when guests arrive. You may substitute canned pineapple for fresh for a simpler family version at home.

1	whole pineapple	3	cups cooked white rice
1½	teaspoons salt, divided	2	tablespoons light soy sauce
	Dash white pepper	1	cup diced cooked shrimp
2	medium eggs, slightly beaten	½	cup small button mushrooms
2	small chicken breasts	½	cup frozen peas, thawed
2	tablespoons vegetable oil, divided	2	green onions, with tops, chopped

Cut the pineapple in half lengthwise and remove the fruit from the middle. Cut out the eyes and core. Set the pineapple shell aside. Dice the pineapple fruit. Dry the diced pineapple with paper towels.

In a medium bowl, add ½ teaspoon salt and the pepper to the eggs.

To cook the chicken breasts, in a medium saucepan, bring 3 cups water to a boil and cook the chicken for about 15 minutes. Cut the cooked chicken into ½-inch diced pieces.

Heat a wok until very hot. Add 1 tablespoon vegetable oil and tilt the wok to coat the sides. Add the eggs. Cook and stir until the eggs are thickened throughout but still moist. Remove the eggs from the wok and set aside. Wash and thoroughly dry the wok.

Make sure all the ingredients are dry before cooking. Reheat the wok until very hot. Add the remaining 1 tablespoon vegetable oil and tilt to coat the sides of the wok. Add the rice and stir-fry for 2 minutes. If you cannot stir-fry fast enough, reduce the heat so the rice will not burn. Stir in the soy sauce and continue stirring until the rice is mixed well with the soy sauce. Stir in the shrimp, chicken, eggs, mushrooms, peas, and the remaining 1 teaspoon salt. Stir-fry for 2 minutes, or until the entire mixture is hot. Stir in the pineapple and green onions.

Rinse the pineapple shell with boiling water; dry with paper towels. Place the pineapple rice into the pineapple shell and serve.

rice bowl with mussels and asparagus

serves 3

This is a wonderful lunch dish or a simple dinner for busy families. Tasty and unique, this recipe is a complete and balanced meal in a bowl.

1	pound mussels
¼	cups red wine
3	to 4 ginger slices
1	ounce fresh shiitake mushrooms
1	pound fresh asparagus
5	cups cooked Jasmine Rice (page 167)
2	tablespoons vegetable oil

1	tablespoon minced garlic
1	teaspoon finely chopped fresh ginger
2	tablespoons oyster sauce
½	teaspoon sugar
¼	cup green onions, with tops, cut into 1-inch pieces

Rinse the mussels under cold water, discarding any mussels with open shells. In a saucepan, put 3 cups water, the wine, and ginger slices and bring to a boil. Add the mussels, cover, and cook for 1 minute over high heat. Remove from the heat. All of the mussels should be opened. Discard any unopened mussels. Remove the mussels from the shell and set aside.

Rinse the shiitake mushrooms with cold water and remove and discard the stems. Pat dry with paper towels. Slice the caps into ½-inch pieces.

Break off the tough ends of the asparagus as far down as the stalks snap easily. Wash well and cut into 2-inch pieces.

Divide the cooked rice among 3 serving bowls and keep warm.

Heat a wok or skillet until hot. Add the vegetable oil, garlic, chopped ginger, mushrooms, and asparagus and stir-fry for 1 minute over high heat. Add the mussels, oyster sauce, sugar, and green onions and continue to stir-fry over high heat for an additional 2 minutes. Turn off the heat, place one third of the stir-fried mixture over each bowl of rice, and serve.

rice noodle salad with ham

You may substitute leftover barbecued pork or chicken or any cooked meat or seafood.

3	to 4 cups vegetable oil	1	tablespoon sugar
2	ounces rice noodles	2	tablespoons white wine vinegar
2	cups shredded ham	2	tablespoons hoisin sauce
½	head shredded iceberg lettuce (about 3 cups)	1	tablespoon sesame oil
1	small shredded carrot (about ½ cup)	1	teaspoon light soy sauce
⅓	cup mayonnaise or salad dressing	1	tablespoon chopped green onion, with tops

Heat the vegetable oil, 1 inch deep, in a wok to 375°F. Fry the noodles, one quarter at a time, about 2 seconds, or until puffed, turning once; drain on paper towels.

In a large bowl, place half of the noodles, the ham, lettuce, and carrot.

In a small bowl, mix together the mayonnaise, sugar, vinegar, hoisin sauce, sesame oil, and soy sauce. Pour the sauce over the ham and vegetables. Top with the remaining noodles and green onion. Toss before serving.

NOTE: The noodles cook very rapidly. Be prepared with a strainer to remove them as soon as they puff up.

roast beef and rice noodles

The beef can be prepared ahead and stored in the freezer. Have rice noodles on hand in your pantry, thaw the beef, and you've got an instant, hearty meal. The total cooking time takes up to 3 hours.

2	pounds beef chuck roast		½	cup red wine or Shaoxing rice wine
1	teaspoon salt		6	whole star anise
¼	teaspoon white pepper		1	tablespoon sugar
2	tablespoons cornstarch		2½	cups Chicken Broth (page 52) or water
3	tablespoons vegetable oil, divided		1	pound wide rice noodles
4	(¼-inch) fresh ginger slices		4	ounces shiitake mushrooms
1	tablespoon minced garlic, divided		2	green onions, chopped
2	tablespoons dark soy sauce			

Cut the roast into 4 pieces. Rub the beef with the salt, pepper, and cornstarch.

In a Dutch oven, heat 2 tablespoons vegetable oil. Place the beef in the pot and brown on both sides. Add the ginger slices, 2 teaspoons garlic, the dark soy sauce, red wine, star anise, and sugar and cook for 1 minute, stirring well. Add the chicken broth or water and bring to a boil. Turn the heat down to medium and cover. Cook about 1 hour and 15 minutes, or until the sauce in the pot equals about 2 cups (add additional water or broth to make 2 cups liquid).

While cooking the beef, in a large saucepan, bring water to a boil. Add the rice noodles and boil for 30 seconds. Drain the noodles and divide them evenly among four bowls.

Rinse the mushrooms with cold water and cut off and discard the stems. Cut the mushroom caps into ½-inch strips. Set aside.

Heat a small skillet over medium heat and add the remaining 1 tablespoon vegetable oil, the remaining 1 teaspoon garlic, and the mushrooms. Stir-fry for 2 minutes and turn off the heat. Place one quarter of the mushroom mixture on top of each bowl of noodles.

When the beef is done, remove it to a platter and let cool. Remove the star anise and ginger slices from the juice and discard. Cut the beef into ¼-inch slices. Place one quarter of the beef slices on each noodle bowl. Pour ½ cup of broth over the beef and garnish with the chopped green onions.

shrimp with garlic noodles

I had never tasted cheese before I came to this country. I learned to like it, but I did not use it in my cooking. On my last visit to Hong Kong, they were using cheese and mayonnaise at one of the upscale restaurants to create very rich-tasting dishes. Since then I've been using these ingredients in some of my own recipes.

8 ounces shrimp (8 to 10 in the shell)	3 teaspoons minced garlic, divided
1⅛ teaspoons salt, divided	1 tablespoon light soy sauce
1 teaspoon cornstarch	½ teaspoon sugar
8 ounces fresh egg noodles (page 163)	1 tablespoon lime juice
5 teaspoons vegetable oil, divided	⅓ cup grated Parmesan cheese

Peel the shrimp. Make a shallow cut lengthwise down the back of each shrimp; wash out the sand vein. In a medium bowl, place warm water and add 1 teaspoon salt; stir to dissolve. Place the shrimp in the salt water and swirl. Leave the shrimp in the salt water for 5 minutes, then rinse with cold water and drain. Pat dry with paper towels. Toss the shrimp with the remaining ⅛ teaspoon salt and the cornstarch to marinate.

In a Dutch oven, bring 2 quarts water to a boil. Add the noodles, stirring to separate. Bring to a boil; reduce the heat to medium. Cook, uncovered, for 1 minute, or until done; drain.

Heat a wok until very hot. Add 1 tablespoon vegetable oil and 2 teaspoons minced garlic. Reduce the heat to medium and add the egg noodles. Stir-fry for about 1 minute, tossing with a fork to separate and cook evenly. Turn off the heat. Add the soy sauce, sugar, and lime juice. Mix in the Parmesan cheese. Place on a platter.

Reheat the wok to very hot and add the remaining 2 teaspoons vegetable oil and 1 teaspoon minced garlic. Add the shrimp and stir-fry for about 2 minutes, or until the shrimp turn pink. Remove the shrimp from the pan and arrange over the top of the noodles. Serve immediately.

soy-flavored rice noodles with beef

6	ounces dried rice noodles		Pinch white pepper	
1	teaspoon sesame oil	4	green onions, with tops	
8	ounces beef sirloin or flank steak	2	tablespoons vegetable oil	
½	teaspoon salt	1	teaspoon minced garlic	
½	teaspoon sugar	2	tablespoons oyster sauce	
1	teaspoon cornstarch			

Soak the rice noodles in warm water for 15 minutes; drain. Rinse with cold water. In a large saucepan, bring 6 cups water to a boil. Add the rice noodles and cook for 30 seconds, stirring to separate. Drain the noodles and mix with the sesame oil. Divide the noodles evenly among 2 bowls and set aside.

Slice the beef very thin and mix together with the salt, sugar, cornstarch, and pepper. Set aside.

Wash and dry the green onions. Cut the green onions into 1-inch pieces.

Heat a 10-inch or larger nonstick skillet over high heat. Add the vegetable oil, beef, and garlic and stir-fry until the beef turns brown, about 1 minute. Push the beef to one side of the pan. Add the rice noodles into the center of the pan, stirring to separate the noodles. Cook the noodles for 1 minute, or until the noodles are hot. Add the green onions and oyster sauce to the noodles. Mix the beef and noodles together, making sure the oyster sauce is mixed throughout all the ingredients in the pan. Serve immediately.

stir-fried pork and broccoli with egg noodles

serves 4

This is a very flexible recipe as you may use any type of meat, vegetable, or noodle for this dish. It is perfect for a fast lunch or dinner.

6   ounces pork loin
¼   teaspoon salt
    Pinch white pepper
2   tablespoons + ½ teaspoon cornstarch, divided
10 ounces broccoli
2   tablespoons oyster sauce

8   ounces dried egg noodles or 14 ounces fresh egg noodles (page 163)
2   tablespoons vegetable oil, divided
2   teaspoons minced garlic
2   tablespoons white wine
1   cup Chicken Broth (page 52)
1   green onion, shredded

Cut the pork into thin strips and mix with the salt, pepper, and ½ teaspoon cornstarch.

Remove the florets from the broccoli, keeping a 1-inch stem. Cut the stems diagonally into ¼-inch slices. In a pot of boiling water, place the broccoli and return to a boil. Cook 1 minute over high heat; drain. Immediately rinse in cold water, drain well, and set aside.

In a small bowl, mix together the remaining 2 tablespoons cornstarch, the oyster sauce, and 2 tablespoons water.

Bring a large pot of water to a boil over high heat. Add the noodles and cook until just al dente, about 5 minutes for dried noodles, 3 minutes for fresh noodles. Drain well and set aside.

Heat a nonstick skillet over high heat. Add 1 tablespoon vegetable oil, the garlic, and noodles and panfry until both sides are browned, about 2 minutes. Place on a plate. Add the remaining 1 tablespoon vegetable oil to the skillet. Add the marinated pork strips and stir-fry until the pork turns white, 1 minute. Add the white wine and stir well. Add the broccoli and chicken broth to the pork strips and heat to boiling. Stir in the cornstarch mixture and cook, stirring constantly, until thickened. Pour the pork and sauce over the noodles. Garnish with the shredded green onion and serve immediately.

stir-fried shrimp with spaghetti noodles

You may substitute any kind of seafood for the shrimp. Cooked leftover seafood may be added at the end of the stir-frying process.

4	teaspoons salt, divided		Pinch white pepper	
8	ounces spaghetti noodles	4	green onions	
6	dried black mushrooms	2	tablespoons vegetable oil	
8	ounces large shrimp	1	teaspoon minced garlic	
½	teaspoon sugar	2	tablespoons oyster sauce	
1	teaspoon cornstarch			

In a Dutch oven, bring 4 quarts water to a boil. Add 2 teaspoons salt. Add the noodles, stirring to separate. Cook for 3 minutes, or until the noodles are done. Drain in a colander.

Soak the mushrooms in hot water until soft, about 20 minutes. Remove and discard the stems; cut the caps into ½-inch strips.

Make a shallow cut lengthwise down the back of each shrimp and wash out the sand vein. In a medium bowl, place warm water and add 1 teaspoon salt; stir to dissolve. Place the shrimp in the salt water and swirl. Leave the shrimp in the salt water for 5 minutes, then rinse with cold water and drain. Pat dry with paper towels. In a bowl, mix the shrimp with the remaining 1 teaspoon salt, sugar, cornstarch, and pepper and set aside.

Wash and dry the green onions. Cut into 1-inch pieces, including the tops.

Heat a wok or large nonstick skillet over high heat. Add the vegetable oil, shrimp, mushrooms, and garlic. Stir-fry until the shrimp turn pink, about 2 minutes. Push the shrimp to one side of the pan. Add the noodles to the pan. Stir the noodles to separate and cook for 1 minute, or until the noodles are hot.

Add the green onions and oyster sauce to the noodles, making sure all the noodles are covered with oyster sauce. Combine the noodles and shrimp and remove to a serving platter.

yeung chau fried rice

Yeung Chau is a province in China known for its superior fried rice dishes. Its name refers to the colorful and tender vegetables that add vibrancy and flavor to this popular recipe. You may enhance this dish by adding cooked meat you have on hand in the refrigerator.

3   tablespoons vegetable oil
1   large egg, slightly beaten
4   cups cooked white rice
½   cup peas
½   cup carrots, cut into ½-inch dice and blanched in boiling water for 1 minute

½   cup diced mushrooms
¾   cup cooked shrimp
¾   cup diced barbecued or cooked chicken
2   green onions, with tops, diced
1   tablespoon oyster sauce

Heat a wok or nonstick skillet over high heat, add the vegetable oil, and stir-fry the egg. Cook the egg to soft scramble. If the rice has just been cooked, fluff with a fork to allow steam to escape and the rice to cool before adding to the wok. After the rice is added, stir constantly and cook for 2 minutes (turn the heat down if the rice starts to stick to the bottom).

Add the peas, diced carrots, diced mushrooms, shrimp, barbecued chicken, green onions, and oyster sauce. Stir until well mixed and the vegetables are hot, about 1 minute. Serve.

desserts

Almond Float with Lychees

Candied Walnuts

Chilled Berry Tea

Eight-Treasure Rice Bowl

Mango Pudding

Lychee Pudding

Poached Peaches with Ginger and Honey

Raspberry Almond Float

Walnut Banana Wontons

Dessert is usually only eaten at banquets in China. This section contains a sampling of authentic banquet-style recipes as well as a few East-meets-West concoctions.

almond float with lychees

This recipe is a variation on a Chinese tofu dessert made long ago. Now you will find tofu desserts at many dim sum restaurants. It can be served with lunch, dinner, or even as a snack. You can also garnish it with your favorite berries along with the light and simple syrup.

1	tablespoon unflavored gelatin	⅛	teaspoon almond extract
2	cups whole milk	8	strawberries, cut into quarters
1½	cups sugar, divided	8	lychees (canned), cut into quarters

In a small bowl, mix ¼ cup cold water with the unflavored gelatin. Stir until completely dissolved.

In a saucepan, place the milk and ½ cup sugar and heat to hot but not boiling. Pour in the gelatin mixture and stir until well mixed. Stir in the almond extract. Pour the mixture into a 9-inch square glass pan and cover with plastic wrap. Chill until firm, about 4 hours or longer.

In a saucepan, place 1 cup water and the remaining 1 cup sugar and bring to a boil. Stir until the sugar is dissolved. Pour over the strawberries and lychees.

Before serving, cut the gelatin in the pan into 1-inch diamond shapes. Pour the strawberry/lychee mixture over the top of the dessert and serve.

candied walnuts

This recipe can be made ahead of time, placed in an airtight container, and used for stir-fried or deep-fried dishes or snacks.

1   pound skinless walnuts
2   cups sugar

2   cups vegetable oil

In a medium saucepan, place 3 cups water and the walnuts and bring to a boil. Add the sugar and boil for 3 minutes. Turn off the heat and let the walnuts soak in the sugar syrup for 2 hours. Drain well and let the walnuts dry for 2 hours. (If you want to hasten the drying process, spread out on a cookie sheet and place in a 350°F. oven for 3 minutes.)

Heat the vegetable oil to 350°F. and deep-fry the walnuts until they are brown, about 1 minute. Be careful not to burn the walnuts. Remove the walnuts and cool completely. Store in an airtight container.

chilled berry tea

serves 6

The combination of star anise and berries is very refreshing after a large dinner. This goes well with any kind of meal.

5   whole star anise (if using broken pieces use
    1 tablespoon)
1¼ cups sugar
2   passion fruit tea bags

3   cups mixed berries (strawberries, blueberries,
    raspberries, blackberries)
½   cup bananas, cut into ½-inch dice

In a saucepan, place 1½ cups water and the star anise, bring to a boil, and cook for 2 minutes. Add the sugar and stir well until the sugar is dissolved. Return to a full boil and turn off the heat. Place the tea bags in the syrup, stir, and let cool. Remove the tea bags and the star anise. Pour the chilled tea over the berries and bananas. Place in the refrigerator until ready to serve.

eight-treasure rice bowl

This dessert is often served after a banquet. It can be served hot or cold, and can be reheated in 3 minutes in the microwave. This dessert needs to be steamed in a 5-cup heat-resistant round-bottomed bowl.

2   cups glutinous rice
2   tablespoons vegetable oil, divided
¼   cup sugar
1½ cups fresh and dried fruit and/or nuts, such as candied cherries, dried blueberries, candied

pineapple, golden raisins, dried mangos, whole walnuts, and mandarin oranges (if canned, drain well)
¾   cup lotus seed paste (7-ounce can)

In a medium bowl, rinse the rice 3 to 4 times with cold water. Cover with cold water and let sit for 10 minutes. Drain well and set aside for 10 minutes.

Heat a large nonstick saucepan over high heat. Add 1 tablespoon vegetable oil and the rice. Stir the rice for about 2 minutes. Add 2 cups cold water, bring to a rolling boil, and cook for 15 seconds over high heat. Cover the pan, reduce the heat to low, and simmer for 20 minutes. Stir in the sugar and mix well.

With a paper towel, wipe the remaining 1 tablespoon vegetable oil over the inside of a 5-cup heat-resistant round-bottomed bowl. Neatly arrange the fruit and nuts in the bottom of the bowl (candied cherries in the center, next circle the dried blueberries around the cherries, and then do the same with the candied pineapple, golden raisins, dried mangos, and whole walnuts, and finally, finish with a ring of mandarin oranges).

Carefully add half of the rice on top of the fruit. Between 2 sheets of wax paper, roll the lotus paste ⅛ inch thick and set over the rice. Add the remaining rice over the lotus paste, gently press down on the rice, and cover with foil.

Place the rice bowl in a steamer and steam over boiling water for 20 minutes. Remove the bowl from the steamer and remove the foil. Place a round platter over the rice and turn the rice bowl upside down on the platter. Carefully lift the bowl off the rice and serve.

mango pudding

Mango pudding has always been a popular dessert in China. This recipe is easy to make and a wonderful after-dinner treat.

1	cup mango (1 large ripe)	1½	tablespoons rum
¾	cup white grape juice, divided	1	tablespoon lime juice
2	teaspoons unflavored gelatin	½	cup heavy cream or sweetened condensed
¾	cup sugar		milk (optional)
½	cup sour cream	8	mint leaves, for garnish (optional)
⅓	cup whole milk		

Peel the skin from the mango and cut the mango off the pit. Cut the mango into 1-inch pieces to yield 1 cup.

In a small bowl, place ¼ cup grape juice. Sprinkle in the gelatin and stir to mix. Let stand for 1 minute. In a small saucepan, heat the remaining ½ cup grape juice until hot. Pour the hot grape juice into the juice/gelatin mixture and stir until the gelatin is completely dissolved. Let cool but not set.

In a blender, place the mango and sugar and blend on high speed until smooth. Add the sour cream, whole milk, rum, lime juice, and gelatin/grape juice mixture and blend well.

Pour into four 8-ounce soufflé dishes. Cover with plastic wrap and chill until firm, about 4 hours or longer.

If desired, this dessert may be served with heavy cream or condensed milk poured over the top and garnished with 2 mint leaves for each serving.

lychee pudding

Lychees are sold in Asian markets and some upscale supermarkets, and they are available in the early summer months.

½ cup white grape juice, divided
1 tablespoon unflavored gelatin
1 cup lychees, drained
1 tablespoon lime juice
½ cup sugar

½ cup sour cream
⅓ cup whole milk
1 tablespoon rum
4 strawberries or cherries, cut in half for garnish

In a small saucepan, place ¼ cup grape juice and heat to hot, not boiling. Sprinkle the gelatin into the remaining ¼ cup grape juice and stir until the gelatin is well mixed. Let stand 1 minute, then stir into the hot grape juice.

In a blender, place the lychees, lime juice, and sugar and blend on high speed until smooth. Add the sour cream, milk, rum, and gelatin/grape juice mixture and blend until the mixture is smooth.

Pour into four 8-ounce soufflé dishes. Cover with plastic wrap and chill 2 hours, then garnish with the strawberry or cherry halves before the pudding becomes too firm. Continue to chill 2 more hours or overnight.

poached peaches with ginger and honey

This dessert is very good to serve after a vegetarian dinner because it is very rich.

6	medium peaches	2	tablespoons cognac (brandy)
1	(1-inch) piece ginger, cut into 4 to 5 thin slices	3	to 4 sprigs mint leaves, for garnish
½	cup sugar	¼	cup roasted slivered almonds
½	cup honey		

In a medium saucepan, bring 2 cups water to a boil. Plunge the peaches into the boiling water and leave for about 30 seconds, then remove and plunge into cold water. Leave for about 3 minutes, remove, and peel the skin with a pointed knife. Cut the peaches in half and remove and discard the pits.

Preheat the oven to 375°F. Place the peach halves in a heatproof baking dish.

In a saucepan, place the ginger slices in water and bring to a boil. Boil for 2 minutes and stir in the sugar. Cook until the sugar is dissolved and add the honey and cognac. Pour the syrup over the peaches. Bake for 30 minutes, turning the peach halves 2 to 3 times to coat the peaches with syrup.

Drain the liquid from the peaches to a saucepan and cook over high heat to reduce the liquid to 1 cup. Pour the sauce over the peaches and garnish with 2 mint leaves and the roasted almonds. Serve hot or cold.

raspberry almond float

*Many years ago when I arrived in this country, I couldn't find soft tofu for this dessert, so I sub-
stituted gelatin to get a similar texture. Now Asian markets carry soft tofu and many tofu desserts.*

1	tablespoon unflavored gelatin	⅛	teaspoon almond extract
2	cups whole milk	2	cups fresh raspberries, rinsed very well
5	tablespoons sugar, divided	8	mint leaves, for garnish

In a small bowl, place ¼ cup water and the unflavored gelatin and stir well to mix.

In a saucepan, place the milk and 1 tablespoon sugar and heat to hot, but not boiling. Pour the gelatin mixture over and stir until the gelatin dissolves. Stir in the almond extract and remove from the heat.

Pour the mixture into a 9-inch square glass pan. Cover with plastic wrap and chill until firm, about 4 hours or longer.

Rinse the raspberries with cold water and drain very well. In a blender or food processor, place the raspberries and the remaining 4 tablespoons sugar and blend until smooth. Strain through a colander to remove the seeds. Pour the sauce on a serving plate and place in the refrigerator to chill.

Before serving, cut the gelatin into 1-inch diamond-shaped pieces and place on top of the raspberry sauce. Garnish with mint leaves and serve.

walnut banana wontons

We usually have fried sweet dumplings for afternoon tea or snacks. This recipe is easy to prepare, since it uses premade wonton wrappers.

2	bananas	20	wonton wrappers
¼	cup Candied Walnuts (page 180)	4	cups vegetable oil for deep-frying
2	tablespoons sugar	¼	cup cinnamon sugar
1	egg, slightly beaten		

Cut the bananas and walnuts into ¼-inch diced pieces. Add the sugar and mix together.

Brush the egg on the edge of a wonton wrapper. Place 2 teaspoons banana mixture in the center of the wonton wrapper. Pull up the 4 corners to the center and pinch together to make a pouch, making sure all the edges are sealed. Repeat the procedure until all the wonton wrappers are made.

In a wok or nonstick skillet, heat the vegetable oil to 350°F. and deep-fry 6 banana wontons at a time. Fry until golden brown. Remove from the oil and immediately sprinkle with cinnamon sugar. Repeat until all the wontons are deep-fried. Serve.

index

conversion chart
Equivalent Imperial and Metric Measurements

American cooks use standard containers, the 8-ounce cup and a tablespoon that takes exactly 16 level fillings to fill that cup level. Measuring by cup makes it very difficult to give weight equivalents, as a cup of densely packed butter will weigh considerably more than a cup of flour. The easiest way therefore to deal with cup measurements in recipes is to take the amount by volume rather than by weight. Thus the equation reads:

1 cup = 240 ml = 8 fl. oz.   ½ cup = 120 ml = 4 fl. oz.

It is possible to buy a set of American cup measures in major stores around the world.

In the States, butter is often measured in sticks. One stick is the equivalent of 8 tablespoons. One tablespoon of butter is therefore the equivalent to ½ ounce/15 grams.

liquid measures

Fluid Ounces	U.S.	Imperial	Milliliters
	1 teaspoon	1 teaspoon	5
¼	2 teaspoons	1 dessertspoon	10
½	1 tablespoon	1 tablespoon	14
1	2 tablespoons	2 tablespoons	28
2	¼ cup	4 tablespoons	56
4	½ cup		120
5		¼ pint or 1 gill	140
6	¾ cup		170
8	1 cup		240
9			250, ¼ liter
10	1¼ cups	½ pint	280
12	1½ cups		340
15		¾ pint	420
16	2 cups		450
18	2¼ cups		500, ½ liter
20	2½ cups	1 pint	560
24	3 cups		675
25		1¼ pints	700
27	3½ cups		750
30	3¾ cups	1½ pints	840
32	4 cups or 1 quart		900
35		1¾ pints	980
36	4½ cups		1000, 1 liter
40	5 cups	2 pints or 1 quart	1120

solid measures

U.S. and Imperial Measures		Metric Measures	
Ounces	Pounds	Grams	Kilos
1		28	
2		56	
3½		100	
4	¼	112	
5		140	
6		168	
8	½	225	
9		250	¼
12	¾	340	
16	1	450	
18		500	½
20	1¼	560	
24	1½	675	
27		750	¾
28	1¾	780	
32	2	900	
36	2¼	1000	1
40	2½	1100	
48	3	1350	
54		1500	1½

oven temperature equivalents

Fahrenheit	Celsius	Gas Mark	Description
225	110	¼	Cool
250	130	½	
275	140	1	Very Slow
300	150	2	
325	170	3	Slow
350	180	4	Moderate
375	190	5	
400	200	6	Moderately Hot
425	220	7	Fairly Hot
450	230	8	Hot
475	240	9	Very Hot
500	250	10	Extremely Hot

Any broiling recipes can be used with the grill of the oven, but beware of high-temperature grills.

equivalents for ingredients

all-purpose flour—plain flour
baking sheet—oven tray
buttermilk—ordinary milk
cheesecloth—muslin
coarse salt—kitchen salt
cornstarch—cornflour
eggplant—aubergine

granulated sugar—caster sugar
half and half—12% fat milk
heavy cream—double cream
light cream—single cream
lima beans—broad beans
parchment paper—greaseproof paper
plastic wrap—cling film

scallion—spring onion
shortening—white fat
unbleached flour—strong, white flour
vanilla bean—vanilla pod
zest—rind
zucchini—courgettes or marrow